No Education
Without Relation

Studies in the
Postmodern Theory of Education

Joe L. Kincheloe and Shirley R. Steinberg
General Editors

Vol. 259

PETER LANG
New York • Washington, D.C./Baltimore • Bern
Frankfurt am Main • Berlin • Brussels • Vienna • Oxford

No Education Without Relation

EDITED BY

Charles Bingham &
Alexander M. Sidorkin

FOREWORD BY

Nel Noddings

PETER LANG
New York • Washington, D.C./Baltimore • Bern
Frankfurt am Main • Berlin • Brussels • Vienna • Oxford

Library of Congress Cataloging-in-Publication Data

No education without relation /
edited by Charles Bingham, Alexander M. Sidorkin.
p. cm. — (Counterpoints; v. 259)
Includes bibliographical references and index.
1. Teacher-student relationships. 2. Communication in education.
I. Bingham, Charles W. (Charles Wayne). II. Sidorkin, Alexander M.
III. Counterpoints (New York, N.Y.); v. 259.
LB1033.N54   371.102'3—dc22   2003018753
ISBN 978-0-8204-6830-3
ISSN 1058-1634

Bibliographic information published by Die Deutsche Bibliothek.
Die Deutsche Bibliothek lists this publication in the "Deutsche
Nationalbibliografie"; detailed bibliographic data is available
on the Internet at http://dnb.ddb.de/.

Cover art by Sharon Bingham
Cover design by Lisa Barfield

The paper in this book meets the guidelines for permanence and durability
of the Committee on Production Guidelines for Book Longevity
of the Council of Library Resources.

© 2004, 2010 Peter Lang Publishing, Inc., New York
29 Broadway, 18th Floor, New York, NY 10006
www.peterlang.com

Printed in the United States of America

TABLE OF CONTENTS

FOREWORD

Nel Noddings

Good teachers have long recognized the central importance of relations in teaching. One can be an effective instructor—one who obtains an impressive number of correct responses from students on tests—without establishing or caring a whit for teacher-student relations. It would be foolish to deny this. Biographical accounts are filled with examples of the useless learning commanded by indifferent, even cruel, instructors. George Orwell, Winston Churchill, and Robert Graves (among many others) have documented both the useless learning and the pedagogical cruelty that often attends it. A teacher, however, is concerned with the development of the persons who are her students. The education that Marie Souvestre provided for Eleanor Roosevelt stands as a model of relational pedagogy. (We may think, too, of the relation established between Anne Sullivan and Helen Keller.) Thus, in some cases, students become successful and decent persons by reacting in opposition to the pedagogy that oppressed them, and in other cases a relational pedagogy opens the way to an intellectually and morally admirable way of life. We know of a few in the first category, but we have no idea how many children have been lost because of pedagogical aloofness or cruelty.

Recognition of the relational nature of teaching should enhance the experience of both students and teachers. The reactions of students invited into a caring relation often include increased interest in the subject matter (if she is interested, it must be worth exploring); enhanced self-esteem (if she sees something in me, I must be worth something); and concern for others (if she cares about them, perhaps I should too). Eleanor Roosevelt and Helen Keller seem to have enjoyed all three of these benefits through the relation with their teachers.

Adopting a philosophy of relational pedagogy also influences teachers' pedagogical choices. Such teachers are likely to accept an internal theory of motivation, one that locates motive energy within the student and his or her interests and purposes, not in external rewards and punishments. They are also likely to vary teaching methods and resist accepting one best way. For example, a teacher who has established a relation with a particular student may understand that the student needs more structure and even coercion than the teacher would like to give. The recognition of relation, not a fixed ideal of teaching, steers the teacher's choice of methods.

Relational pedagogy requires teachers to acquire much broader competence in a variety of subjects. Knowing that they will meet students with widely varying interests, teachers must continue to learn and to share their learning in response to the expressed needs of students. This mutual benefit—enhanced learning for both teacher and student—is an important product of relational pedagogy.

Still another benefit may be a deeper, more genuine appreciation of democracy. When we take the time to establish relations of care and trust, we learn that some students will probably never acquire a real understanding of our subject. At the same time, we learn that these students have talents and skills that we will not acquire. This situation does not imply a failure of either student or teacher but an opportunity for mutual respect. Over the years, in working with students whose interests have varied enormously, I have become more and more deeply aware of our social interdependence. Democracy does not require that everyone have an education exactly like mine. On the contrary, it requires—as John Dewey and Walt Whitman saw clearly—that all individual talents be cultivated and all honest work be appropriately compensated.

Readers of this book will see that advocates of relational pedagogy do not agree entirely on how to define it. You will find here a variety of interpretations, different emphases, and a host of fascinating questions.

Finally, it should be noted that educational theorists are not alone in exploring and analyzing relational views. It is gratifying to see similar efforts growing in law, medicine, social work, nursing, religion, psychology, feminist studies, peace studies, and even physics. Exploration of relations ranges from highly abstract ontological discussions to the ultimately practical concerns of teaching. You will find some of both here.

ACKNOWLEDGMENTS

This book was made possible because of the support of the National Academy of Education and the Spencer Foundation. The editors thank Professor Nel Noddings for her critique of the earlier version of the book. We also would like to acknowledge the profound influence Professor Donna Kerr has had on the editors and some of the authors. We would like acknowledge Marela Dichupa for extensive help in editing this volume.

THE PEDAGOGY OF RELATION: AN INTRODUCTION

Charles Bingham and
Alexander M. Sidorkin

This book was conceived as a collective statement about a new approach in educational theory. It presents an emerging concept, the concept of relational pedagogy. Educational thought in the twentieth century was puzzled by many challenges. One of them could be described as follows: If, in education, one moves away from universal claims, then education might rather become sensitive to the particular. But how can one understand and describe something, in any comprehensive way, as the particular? This challenge has special significance for an applied discipline such as education. As an applied discipline, educational theory needs to be useful. One cannot simply tell educators, "Just pay attention to the particulars; it all depends on context." One needs to provide educators with a theory that can be helpful. The concept of relations, if properly developed, can serve as a more useful educational tool than those that have been developed around the vast array of human particularities. What we offer is not a statement such as, "It all depends on the particulars," but rather, "It all depends on relations." Relations can be clearly analyzed and described to the benefit of educators.

Like many "new" approaches, the pedagogy of relation is not actually new at all. Although Frank Margonis, one of our authors, may probably claim the authorship to the exact words "pedagogy of relation," it would be most unfair to suggest that scholars before us have paid no attention to the relational side of education. There is a long philosophical tradition of emphasizing relations, starting with Aristotle. Among the most obvious recent sources, one can mention Buber, Bakhtin, Dewey, Gadamer, and Heidegger. This volume was not intended to explore the theoretical sources of the pedagogy of relation. We will indeed refer to the work done by Nel Noddings, who put relational thinking into the mainstream of American educational theory.[1] She, along with a few others, has most explicitly created the tradition of concentrating on relation both in ethics and in educational theory. Examples of theoretical constructs that take human relationships to be the primary building blocks of reality are Noddings's examination of care, Martin's idea of the Schoolhome, and Carol Gilligan's feminist ethics. In its own way, critical pedagogy also explores the interplay between socially determined and interhuman relations, especially as it is developed by Paulo Freire. Educational scholars focusing on a communicative approach also belong to this group. We wanted to revisit a number of existing conversations and bring together several theoretical traditions under the umbrella of the pedagogy of relation. This volume is thus a collection of viewpoints on relation, but also an appeal to develop a common frame of reference for these and other approaches. Its chapters are all based on the assumption that relations have primacy over the isolated self.

The various authors of this book have been in conversation with one another for quite a few years. At some point, we realized that despite many differences in our approaches and orientations, we all take the notion of relations very seriously. The authors of this book try to understand human relations rather than educational processes, behaviors, methods, curriculum, and so on. We are interested in how interhuman relations affect and define teaching and learning. The organizing concept of this book is thus the concept of relation. Each author contributes to the central premise that meaningful education is possible only when relations are carefully understood and developed.

We develop the pedagogy of relation because of practical concerns about education. The extensive Claremont study defined the main issues affecting American public education as seen from inside the classroom—by students, teachers, parents, and administrators. The number one issue turned out to be that of relationships. "Participants feel the crisis inside schools is directly linked to human relationships. This theme was prominently stated by participants and so deeply connected to all other themes in the data that it is believed this may be one of the two most central issues in solving the crisis inside schools."[2] This study shows that there is a very practical need for relational educational theory that would penetrate the world of practical teachers' thinking and mainstream policy making.

This need is growing especially urgent in the context of a continuing wave of educational reform centered on accountability and academic achievement. The "Era of Excellence" in American education began in the early 1980s and shows no signs of ending. One of the main assumptions of this reform is that in order to be effective, schools must concentrate on their primary mission— teaching academic skills and content. This logic borrowed from the world of business may not be applicable to schools. This academic "purification" of educational purposes tends to destroy the already fragile layers of public education conducive to development of flourishing human relations. And ironically, once the relational basis of a school organization is destroyed or severely limited, it becomes more and more difficult to achieve high academic standards. This concern goes well beyond the abstract discourse about the purposes of public education. Even the most narrowly construed "back to basics" purposes of public schooling may become unachievable if schools lose the ability to foster human relationships that allow them to function. In other words, even in a technicist approach to education such as the one that currently has a stranglehold on many educational institutions, it might be conceded that educational relations are paramount. But this book is not meant to offer a pragmatic orientation that would foster academic achievement. On the contrary, it proposes that results are a means to relation rather than the other way around.

Unlike many other edited collections, this book was written with considerable collaborative effort. The core group of authors formed a number of symposia to air initial ideas and to solicit feedback from colleagues. In addition, most of the authors attended a retreat in the spring of 2002, where the text of the "Manifesto of Relations" was developed. Because of this additional work many chapters refer to each other, and challenge, critique, and develop each other's positions.

This book opens with the Manifesto, which presents a number of claims about educational theory, about relationality, and about the pedagogy of relations. The chapters are broken into three parts. Part I outlines the theoretical territory for the new approach and positions it among the existing conversations. Biesta and Sidorkin are concerned with outlining the theoretical territory for the pedagogy of relation; the former links it to the theory of communicative education, and the latter to economic anthropology. Margonis offers a compelling case study that presents the promise of this pedagogy. Bingham takes a new look at educational authority, informed by the notion of relational pedagogy.

The four chapters of Part II are oriented around democratic engagement. Hutchinson considers the notion of narrative and links the pedagogy of relation to democracy. Both Lyon McDaniel and Pijanowski bring a psychoanalytic dimension to our conversation, and they show how the notion of care may or may not be applied in education. Mayo mounts a critical challenge to the perspective of care. She argues that family cannot serve as a model for meaningful educational relations. Both Hutchinson and Lyon McDaniel consider relations with strangers and their implications for democracy.

The authors in Part III explore the epistemological and curricular implications of relational pedagogy. Thayer-Bacon gives an overview of relational epistemology. Romano develops a concept of literacy that involves knowledge of social relations. Stengel gives a fascinating account of one child's learning within different relational contexts.

The book does not present a complete theory of educational relations. However, it maps out important potential conversations and invites others to participate.

Notes

1. See, for example, Nel Noddings, *Caring: A Feminine Approach to Ethics and Moral Education* (Berkeley: University of California Press, 1984) and Nel Noddings, *Women and Evil* (Berkeley: University of California Press, 1989).
2. Mary Poplin and Joseph Weeres, eds., *Voices from the Inside: A Report on Schooling Inside the Classroom. Part One: Naming the Problem* (Claremont, CA: The Institute for Education in Transformation at the Claremont Graduate School, 1992).

MANIFESTO OF RELATIONAL PEDAGOGY: MEETING TO LEARN, LEARNING TO MEET

A joint contribution by all authors

A fog of forgetfulness is looming over education. Forgotten in the fog is that education is about human beings. And as schools are places where human beings get together, we have also forgotten that education is primarily about human beings who are in relation with one another.

Why do schools remain if not for meeting? The very existence of schools is surprising. In this age of books, libraries, TV, DVDs, and computers, schools are not the only place to get information. People are really in a position to teach themselves. Yet there are still elementary schools, there are still secondary schools, and there are still colleges and universities.

Why do schools remain? They remain because education is not mainly about the facts that students stuff into their heads. They remain because education is not mainly about developing thinking skills. It is not about gaining knowledge. Schools remain because education is primarily about human beings who need to meet together, as a group of people, if learning is to take place. In schools, it is true that we meet and it is true that we learn. But the fog over education has kept us from realizing that learning is primarily about human beings who meet. Meeting and learning are inseparable.

So the fog must rise. We must learn to meet. Why? Because we must meet to learn. We are shifting the spotlight from individuals, groups, and their practices onto relations.

Historical Turning Point

The remarkable growth of schooling in the twentieth century has shaken the very foundation of education. For centuries, schools could enforce order by selecting some and excluding others. With the advent of mass compulsory schooling and the struggle for equal access to education, the exclusion or threat of exclusion can no longer be used to hold schools together. The situation is paradoxical and potentially dangerous: The information-based economy requires higher and higher levels of education of a larger and larger proportion of the population. At the same time, school authority is quickly losing its power over the lives of students.

Another development has been the birth of large, bureaucratic, and highly organized school organizations. This is another attempt to address the massification of schooling by using known economic models.

The loss of control and bureaucratization of schools has created a growing problem of alienation. Students, teachers, and parents increasingly find themselves in situations void of meaningful human contact, ridden with frustration and anonymity. This is the cause of the widespread dissatisfaction with schooling. The low expectations, breakdown of social order, and academic failure are only symptoms of the much deeper problem of alienation. Simply put, students and teachers cannot and will not do a good job within discouraging and alienating schools.

To patch up the alienation problem, traditionalists and Progressivists offer two different solutions. The traditionalists want to return to more exclusionary, but more orderly, schools. They demand high-stake tests and accountability. These measures will inevitably make schools less inclusive, but it is doubtful that they will restore the social order, not to mention address alienation. The Progressivists still believe that reformed curriculum and engaged instruction can awaken intrinsic motivation in all children, and thus make schools more interesting and less alienating. This solution is idealistic, because it expects all children to be interested in learning.

We offer a third solution. It relies on neither brute force of exclusion nor on romantic expectations. Schools must focus on human relations and address the core of the problem. A school with a vibrant community can avoid dangerous outbursts of vandalism and violence. Such a school can also compensate for the lack of intrinsic motivation, because students learn partially out of respect for teachers and peers.

The pedagogy of relation will not necessarily solve the problems of inequality and prejudice that plague our schools. However, we need to move from struggling against something to struggling for something. pedagogy of relation offers an ideal of school based on the notion of democratic relations.

Relational Propositions

Therefore, the following principles of relation are acknowledged:
— A relation is more real than the things it brings together. Human beings and non-human things acquire reality only in relation to other beings and things.

— The self is a knot in the web of multiple intersecting relations; pull relations out of the web, and find no self. We do not have relations; relations have us.

— Authority and knowledge are not something one has, but relations, which require others to enact.

— Human relations exist in and through shared practices.

— Relations are complex; they may not be described in single utterances. To describe a relation is to produce a multivoiced text.

— Relations are primary; actions are secondary. Human words and actions have no authentic meaning; they acquire meaning only in a context of specific relations.

— Teaching is building educational relations. Aims of teaching and outcomes of learning can both be defined as specific forms of relations to oneself, people around the students, and the larger world.

— Educational relation is different from any other; its nature is transitional. Educational relation exists to include the student in a wider web of relations beyond the limits of the educational relation.

— Relations are not necessarily good; human relationality is not an ethical value. Domination is as relational as love.

PART 1

PEDAGOGY OF RELATION:
MAPPING THE TERRITORY

"MIND THE GAP!" COMMUNICATION AND THE EDUCATIONAL RELATION

Gert Biesta

The relation between teachers and students can be understood as a process of communication. But what is communication? How does it take place? And what kind of relation between teachers and students is established through communication? Many people would argue that education is about the transfer of knowledge, skills, values, attitudes, and dispositions from the teacher to the student. Although this may be an accurate (though very limited) description of what goes on between teachers and students, it doesn't provide an understanding of how this is actually possible. In this chapter I discuss three theories of communication in order to explore how communication between students and teachers is possible. Rather than thinking of communication as a direct relation between teachers and students, I argue that there is a gap between the teacher and the student. This gap is a necessary condition for communication—and hence education—to take place. A pedagogy of relation should, therefore, acknowledge and affirm the uncertainties and risks *and* the possibilities that are at stake in this gap.

The Location of Education

"Do we have a theory of education?" At first sight this may be an odd question to ask. Educators and educational researchers would presumably say that we have many theories of education. But everything depends on what we actually mean by a theory of education and, even more, what we mean by "education." My concern in this chapter, however, is not so much with the definition of education, as with the question of where education takes place; the question, in other words, of the *location* of education.

When we look at the theories that are available in the field of education, we have, on the one hand, a whole range of theories that focus on the one who does the educating. These involve teaching, instruction, training, parenting, and guiding. From a historical point of view it can even be argued that for a long time "education" meant nothing but the kind of activities implied by such theories. Education was conceived in terms of what an educator (a teacher, a parent, an instructor, a tutor) did. On the other hand, the field of education has a whole range of theories about learning, development, change, formation, and transformation. These theories try to articulate what takes place on the side of the "recipient" of education. In the history of Western education, Rousseau can be credited as one of the first to emphasize the fact that the recipient of education is not some sort of passive material that can simply be molded in any way the educator wants. The most recent recognition of the active role of the recipient of education can be found in the many varieties of constructivism that are currently being proposed in educational psychology and educational epistemology. We also shouldn't forget the ideas of progressive educators such as Dewey in the United States, Kerschensteiner in Germany, or Ligthartt in the Netherlands, who all made the case that the activities of the learner are a crucial and constitutive dimension of any educative process. Just as it takes two to tango, it takes (at least) two for education to happen.

When we take our cue from theories that are available in the field of education, we can see that we have theories about the activities of the educator and theories about the activities of the one who is being educated (a child, a student, a learner). Between the two there is a *gap*. It could be argued—and many people indeed do argue this—that education is the *interaction* between the activities of the educator and the activities of the one being educated. It could further be argued—and again there are many who do so—that the ultimate aim of education is to narrow, bridge, or close the gap between the (activities of the) educator and the (activities of the) one being educated. The idea here is that successful education is the situation where the activities of the educator determine the activities of the one being educated; that teaching, in other words, should control learning. Such a causal conception of education lies behind notions of effective teaching and effective schooling. It is exemplified in a whole research tradition that tries to identify the factors that determine learning. And it is the logic behind the idea that education can be used as a means to bring about predetermined ends, ends such as the fostering of moral persons, obedient citizens, or a stable society.

The idea that education is an interaction between the (activities of the) educator and the (activities of the) one being educated is, as such, a sound idea. It shows that education is basically a *relationship* between an educator and the one being educated. But in order to understand the precise nature of the educational relationship, we should take the idea that education consists of the interaction between the teacher and the learner absolutely seriously. We should take it in its most literal sense. If we do so, it follows that education is located not in the activities of the teacher, nor in the activities of the learner, but in the interaction between the two. Education, in order words, takes place in the gap between the teacher and the learner.

If this is the location of education, if this is where education literally "takes place," then a theory of education should be a theory about the *interaction* between the teacher and the student. A theory of education is, in other words, a theory about the educational relationship. It is *not* about the "constituents" of this relationship (i.e., the teacher and the learner) but about the "relationality" of the relationship. I do not think that we already have many such theories, and perhaps we do not even have any at all. The purpose of this chapter is to develop such a theory, or at least to make clear in outline what such a theory might look like. I will approach this task, as mentioned previously, by discussing three theories of communication. This, so I will argue, will help us to understand that the gap between the teacher and the student is not something that should be overcome, because it is this very gap that makes communication—and hence education—possible.

Model 1: Communication as the Transmission of Information

The most widespread theory of communication, and the one that appeals most to commonsense ideas about communication, is the so-called "sender-receiver" model of communication,[1] which is also known as the "information-theoretical" model of communication.[2] In this model, communication is conceived as the transmission of information from one place (the sender) to another place (the receiver) through a medium or channel. It includes processes of encoding on the side of the sender in order to put the information in such a form that it can go through the medium or channel. It involves processes of decoding on the side of the receiver in order to transform the encoded information back into its original state. A paradigm-case of the sender-receiver model is television broadcasting, where information (images and sounds) produced in a studio is transferred to the television sets in the homes of viewers through a process of encoding and decoding.

While the sender-receiver model might be an adequate way to describe the transmission of bits of information through a medium, it is an inadequate model for the description of human communication. The main reason is that human communication is not about information but about meaning. The sender-receiver model provides a perfect description of the transportation of images and sounds from point A to point B, but it forgets that we also need someone who actually watches the TV, someone who actually *makes sense* of the images and sounds. The problem with the sender-receiver model, to put it differently, is that it assumes that the meaning of the information is attached to the information itself. As soon as we see, however, that meaning is not something that we passively receive, but rather something that we actively (though not necessarily always consciously) ascribe to something—we *give* meaning to, we *make* sense of—it becomes clear that the sender-receiver model omits the most crucial part of human communication, viz., the interpretation of the message on the side of the receiver. What is sent, in other words, never determines what is received. Or, to put it in more practical terms: In human communication it is always possible that what a speaker or a writer (or, for that matter, a teacher or a lecturer) means by the information he or she provides is interpreted in completely different ways by various listeners, readers, and students.

One can of course try to "repair" this model by introducing feedback. The sender and the receiver change roles, so that the receiver can return her interpretation to the sender in order to check whether the way in which she understood the information is similar to what the sender intended to say. Feedback, however, cannot solve the fundamental problem of the sender-receiver model, because just as the receiver has to make sense of what is being sent, the sender, in turn, has to make sense of what is returned to her by the receiver. I am not arguing that feedback makes no sense in the day-to-day practice of communication. But there is a limit to what feedback can achieve. Teachers know all too well that although students might *say* that they have understood the lesson, and may even be able to return the whole lesson to the teacher in the very words in which the lesson was taught, it can still turn out that they haven't understood it at all. "Do you really understand what I mean?" "Yes." "Really?" "Really!" "Really 'really'?" *Et ad infinitum.*

One reason why the sender-receiver model is unhelpful for understanding communication is that it basically is a black-box model: It describes the relationship between the input and output of communication, but doesn't provide an explanation of the process itself. What also shouldn't be forgotten is that the sender-receiver model is a normative model of communication in that it relies on a very specific idea of what successful communication is, viz., the situation in which the input and output of communication are identical. According to this model, successful communication is communication without change, without interpretation, without creativity. Successful communication is nothing but repetition. The use of the sender-receiver model in understanding education is therefore limited to those cases in which the aim of education is itself understood as faithful and obedient repetition.

Model 2: Communication as Participation

Given the discussion so far, the question that needs to be addressed is how communication of meaning is possible. In trying to answer this question, we must keep in mind that interpretation is central to human communication. We do not passively receive meaning, but actively *give* meaning to and *make* sense of what we encounter. One way, therefore, to approach this question is to ask how, in the case of education, the child, the learner, or the student can get access to the meanings that are available in a culture or a subsystem of a culture (such as the meanings embodied in science, religion, mathematics, history, language, etc.).

Let's take a simple example. How can a child learn the meaning of a traffic light? The way in which children normally try to make sense of the environment in which they live is by means of experimentation—which, in the case of children, we tend to call "play." The basic pattern of experimentation is that we do something, we interact with the objects in our environment, and we undergo the consequences of what we do. By experimenting with the traffic light, a child can discover many different things. She can, for instance, discover that it is possible to climb up the traffic light and use it as a lookout. She can discover a pattern in the change of the colors and can get aesthetic pleasure out of it. She can even discover interesting wires and switches inside the traffic light. But the only thing the child cannot discover by means of his or her own individual experimental interaction with the traffic light is the meaning that the traffic light plays in the regulation of traffic. This is because such meaning does not exist in the traffic light itself, i.e., in the "thingness" of the traffic light. The meaning of the traffic light exists only in the way in which people use traffic lights to coordinate their actions. The meaning of the traffic light exists, in other words, only in the social practice in which the traffic light plays a role. Stated in more precise terms, the meaning does not exist in the heads or bodies of the individuals who make up the social practice, but rather is located *in between* them. This suggests that the only way in which a child can gain access to the meaning that exists in social practices is by taking part in these practices and, by doing so, becoming part of them. How can we understand this process? What, in other words, is the "mechanism" of participation?

A detailed answer to this question can be found in the writings of John Dewey and George Herbert Mead. They have developed an understanding of communication in thoroughly practical terms, i.e., as a process in which, through the coordination of action, meanings are shared and a common world is brought into existence.[3] The place to begin in understanding this theory is to acknowledge that we basically all have our own idiosyncratic view of the world. For each of us the world in which we live and work has a unique, individual meaning that is the result of our past experiences and our past learning. As long as we do not interact with other human beings, the fact that we live and work in different worlds is not really a problem. As soon, however, as we begin to act together, that is, when we engage in a common activity in order to achieve something together, it becomes important for the successful coordination of our activities that we "see" or "approach" the world in a sufficiently similar way. Or to be more precise: that we see and give meaning to relevant dimensions of the world in a sufficiently similar way.

The point of Dewey's and Mead's understanding of human cooperation is not, however, that we should first agree about our interpretation of the world and only then start our common activity. Their point is that the change of our individual perspectives is the result of our attempts to coordinate our actions and activities. We continuously make minor adjustments in our own understandings, our own ways of responding, our own ways of seeing, in order to bring about coordinated action. Dewey argues that we should understand communication in precisely this way, i.e., as "the establishment of cooperation in an activity in which there are partners, and in which the activity of each is modified and regulated by partnership."[4] Communication is the making of something in common. It is important to note that making something "in common" does not imply that the understandings of person A and person B become identical. The process is one of the construction of a shared understanding, an understanding or outlook or perspective that is the shared "possession" of the partners in interaction.

If we apply this theory of communication to our example of the traffic light, we can see that successful participation in the social practice in which the traffic light plays a role would require that the child adjust his or her initial perspective in such a way and to such an extent that cooperation with others becomes possible. It is not that the child first has to change her perspective in order *then* to be able to take part in the practice. The adjustment is *both the condition and the result* of successful participation. It is important to see that this is not a one-way process in which the child simply has to adjust herself to the existing conditions. Although there is a practical limit to the amount of change that a practice can afford, it is clear that as soon as a child (or another newcomer) starts to take part in a practice, the practice will already have changed. Even more: As soon as newcomers begin to take part, those who made up the practice up to that point will also need to respond, and hence to adjust themselves and their outlook to the newcomers. It is in this way that participation results in the construction of *shared* understanding and *shared* world—which, to emphasize this point one more time, is *not* an identical world for all who take part in it.

Education as Participation

Now we should take some care to flesh out the significance of the participatory model for education. The participatory theory of communication provides an interesting answer to the question of how the communication of meaning is possible. Its basic premise is that meaning only exists in social practices, which means that it is located *in between* the individuals who constitute the social practice through their interactions. This implies that communication is not about the transportation of meaning, but about participation, coordination, co-construction, and transformation. The participatory understanding of communication entails, in other words, a completely different vocabulary in which questions about transportation, transmission, or transfer are simply meaningless. One of the most important conclusions to be drawn from this theory of communication is that the transformation of meaning is not the exception, it is not a disturbance of successful communication, but rather the very "mechanism" through which the communication of meaning takes place. It is the mechanism that makes communication possible. This is not to suggest that misunderstanding is the rule of all communication. It only means that communication works through difference and change and not through identity and stability.

If it is the case that meaning only exists *in* social practices, then it also follows that meaning can only be (re)presented in and through social practices. For education this implies, among other things, that we should think of the curriculum as a representation of practices inside the walls of the school, and not as a representation of formal abstractions from these practices. It would, for example, mean that the teaching of mathematics should be about bringing the practice of mathemat*izing* into the school and allowing for students to take part in this practice, just as, for example, the teaching of history should be about the practice of *historicizing*.

The educational implications of the participatory theory of communication are not only programmatic. The idea that students learn from the practices in which they engage is also helpful in understanding why something like the hidden curriculum is so effective—and often more effective than the official curriculum. The hidden curriculum, defined as that which is implicitly learned by students rather than what is explicitly taught, is located in the very practices in which children and students take part during their time in school, while the official curriculum is much more an artificial add-on to the real "life in schools." This also explains why one of the things that children and students learn most effectively during their time in schools or other educational institutions is how to "survive" their school. Schooling is first and foremost, so we could say, a socialization into the culture of schooling itself.

The participatory theory of communication also has implications for the way in which we think about the "gap" between the teacher and the student. According to the transmission model of communication, the gap between the teacher and the student can only be understood as a hindrance for the efficient and effective flow of information from the teacher to the student. This explains why educators and educational theorists who rely on this model see the gap as a problem that should be overcome. What the participatory theory of communication suggests is that the gap is not something that is alien to the process of communication, but rather something that belongs to it, something that makes communication possible. According to the participatory theory there is, after all, no direct effect of the teacher on the student, but only an indirect one. Teaching is not some kind of "input" that ideally should go directly into the mind of the student without any noise, disturbance, or transformation. Teaching is about the construction of a social situation, and the effects of teaching result from the activities of the students in and in response to this social situation. (This is true even for those cases in which the teacher would do all the talking and the student would only be "allowed" to listen and make notes.) The gap between teacher and learner is crucial for education. It belongs to education and makes it possible. Trying to close or do away with the gap is, therefore, a mistake.

We can take this point a bit further and ask the question, Who actually educates? Common sense would dictate that educators educate—and in a certain sense this is, of course, true. But if it is the case that there is no direct relationship between the activities of the educator and the learning of the student, but that instead learners learn from their participation in a social situation, then the conclusion has to be that it is the social situation that emerges from the interaction between the teacher and student that actually "does" the education. In this respect we can say not only that education happens in the gap between the teacher and the student. We might even say that it is this gap itself that educates.

Model 3: A Performative Theory of Communication

Although the third model of communication that I want to discuss isn't in contradiction with the participatory approach, it does provide the opportunity for a refinement of some of the ideas of the participatory model and, in doing so, results in a theory that in a certain respect is more consistent than the participatory approach. This model, the *performative* theory of communication, also allows for a more precise understanding of the nature of the gap between the teacher and the student.

We have seen that one of the central ideas of the participatory theory of communication lies in the claim that meaning exists only in the *in-between* space that is brought about by human interaction. From this, two conclusions follow. Firstly, if it is the case that meaning exists only in an in-between space constituted by communication, then it follows that the existence of meaning is dependent on its continuous reproduction in and through communication.

Throughout history many devices have been developed to record, store, and preserve meaning. But these devices can store only traces of meaning, not the meaning itself. We can create many cultural artifacts, but without the cultural practices in which these artifacts have meaning, there is no way of preserving the meaning invested in the artifacts. Cultural artifacts without practices remain silent—a problem that archeologists are all too familiar with. This fact implies not only that meaning, and culture more generally, exist only in and through communication. Since communication is basically a process of transformation, it also means that the "mechanism" for the preservation of meaning and culture is itself transformatory. Contrary to what many would like to think, meaning and culture can endure only in transformation.

Secondly, if it is conceded that meaning exists only in and through communication, then we are moving away from an *epistemological* understanding of meaning in which meaning is seen as the representation of something outside of the sphere of communication (something that Derrida would call a "transcendental signifier"). What an utterance means, in other words, is not secured or safeguarded by its reference to something outside of the sphere of communication, but depends crucially on the process of communication itself. What we have here, then, is an approach in which the "performance" of meaning in communication is central. It is an approach that focuses on the "enunciation" of meaning.[5] Homi Bhabha describes the shift from an epistemological understanding of meaning and culture to an understanding of culture as an "enunciative practice" as follows.

> If culture as epistemology focuses on function and intention, then culture as enunciation focuses on signification and institutionalization; if the epistemological tends towards a reflection of its empirical referent or object, the enunciative attempts repeatedly to reinscribe and relocate the political claim to cultural priority and hierarchy (high/low, ours/theirs) in the social institution of the signifying activity. The epistemological is locked into the hermeneutic circle, in the description of cultural elements as they tend towards a totality. The enunciative is a more dialogic process that attempts to track displacements and realignments that are the effects of cultural antagonisms and articulations—subverting the rationale of the hegemonic moment and relocating alternative, hybrid sites of cultural negotiation.[6]

What is at stake in the shift from representation to enunciation is that meaning is radically placed *inside* the process of communication. Since communication is a transformative process, this means that the transformation of meaning should be thought of as the normal course of events in all communication. As Bhabha puts it:

> Translation is the performative nature of cultural communication. It is language in actu (enunciation, positionality) rather than language in situ (énoncé, or propositionality).

And the sign of translation continually tells, or "tolls" the different times and spaces
between cultural authority: cultural and its performative practices[7]

The theory of communication that emerges from these ideas is one in
which the gap between those who take part in communication plays a crucial
role. Bhabha refers to this gap as the "Third Space of enunciation."[8] This Third
Space is neither me/where I am, nor you/where you are. It is precisely the *in-
between* that makes any communication and any existence of meaning possible.
To quote Bhabha once more:

> The act of interpretation is never simply an act of communication between the I and
> the You designated in the statement. The production of meaning requires that these
> two places be mobilized in the passage through a Third Space, which represents both
> the general conditions of language and the specific implications of the utterance in a
> performative and institutional strategy of which it cannot "in itself" be conscious. What
> this unconscious relation introduces is an ambivalence in the act of interpretation…
> The meaning of the utterance is quite literally neither the one nor the other.[9]

Bhabha's point here is that the Third Space, the gap in which enunciation
"takes place," makes the "transfer" of meaning into an ambivalent and transformative process. Yet this ambivalence is not something that can be overcome.
It is a necessary condition of all communication. But if this is the case, then it
also follows that the gap, the Third Space, can itself no longer be represented in
any positive sense. The only way to represent the gap is in and through communication. While I would be able to tell you what I think the gap consists of, I
can in no way control the meaning that my utterance will have in the space of
enunciation. In this respect the gap is elusive but at the same time very real. As
Bhabha summarizes:

> It is that Third Space, though unrepresentable in itself, which constitutes the discursive
> conditions of enunciations that ensure that the meaning and symbols of culture have
> no primordial unity or fixity; that even the same signs can be appropriated, translated,
> rehistoricized and read anew.[10]

The unrepresentability of the gap or Third Space suggests an important difference between the performative theory of communication and the participatory theory. One could argue that the participatory theory of communication
still assumes that it is possible to represent the "mechanism" of communication
from some (philosophical) place outside the process of communication. Bhabha
provides us with an outlook on communication that, in a sense, folds its own
understanding back on itself. His approach suggests that a theory of communication is itself subjected to the transformative logic of communication. It can, in

other words, only be enunciated in communication but never represented from a position outside of the sphere of communication.

Conclusions: Teaching in the Gap

In this chapter I have presented three different theories of communication in order to explore the intuition with which I began—that education takes place in the interaction between the teacher and the learner. My initial question was whether we have a theory of education. In a sense my paradoxical answer has to be that ultimately we cannot have a theory of education. The gap in which education takes place is, after all, ultimately unrepresentable. But although we cannot represent the gap in any positive sense, and in this sense cannot have a theory of education, this doesn't mean that we can simply forget about the gap. The unrepresentability of what makes education possible, rather, highlights the performative nature of the process of education, that is, the fact that education exists only in and through the communicative interaction between the teacher and the learner. It highlights, in other words, the enuciative nature of all education. This is a more precise way to understand the point I made earlier that it is the gap itself that actually educates.

This also gives us a better understanding of the relationality of the educational relationship. It helps us first of all to understand that education has indeed a relational character, that it doesn't exist in any other sense than as a relation and "in relation." But this relation is not one where there is a direct input from the teacher into the mind of the student. The relation is only possible because of the existence of an unrepresentable, transformative gap, a space of enunciation that cannot be controlled by any of the partners in interaction, but at the very same time makes communication possible. This helps us to see that there is no relation in education without the separation brought about by the gap. Educational relations are, in other words, never direct, nor are they simple.

Does anything more practical than a better understanding of the process of education and the educational relationship follow from all this? Perhaps it does (and I want to credit the students whom I taught about these ideas for helping me to understand the possible practical meaning of my ideas). One could argue that, in a sense, teachers have two options. They can negate the gap and act as if their task is to impact directly upon the minds of their students—and to the extent that they are not successful or effective in doing so, they can blame either themselves or their students. (In many countries, governments have decided that this should be the daily reality for teachers and students.) Or teachers can acknowledge the existence of the gap as a space of enunciation that is brought into existence only as a result of the common effort of teachers and learners, a space that exists only in communication. To go into the gap, to "descend into that alien territory,"[11] entails both a risk and an opportunity. The risk is clear: The space of enunciation is in a very fundamental and practical sense unpredictable. Yet it is at the same time the space in which speaking becomes possible; it is the space, in other words, where people—individual, singular beings—can reveal who they are, can come "into presence." This is the opportunity provided by the space of enunciation, by the gap between the teacher and the student. It is the opportunity of agency, both, so I want to emphasize, for the student and the teacher. This is not the agent-subject that exists before the social. Nor is this the agent-subject that needs to be liberated or emancipated by the teacher. The agency that becomes possible in the gap is a fragile "enunciative agency."[12] It is a concern for the possibility of this enunciative agency to happen that, I believe, is the most important practical conclusion that can be drawn from the foregoing exercise. It is what makes the risk of teaching in the gap worthwhile and, so I believe, necessary.

Notes

1. See D. McQuail and S. Windahl, "Models of Communication," in *International Encyclopedia of Communication*, eds. E. Barnouw, G. Gerbner, W. Schramm, T. L. Worth, and L. Gross (New York/Oxford: Oxford University Press, 1989), 36.

2. See Klaus Schaller, *Pädagogik der Kommunikation. Annäherungen. Erprobungen* (Sankt Augustin: Richarz, 1987).

3. For a more detailed account see Gert J. J. Biesta, "Pragmatism as a Pedagogy of Communicative Action," in *The New Scholarship on John Dewey*, ed. Jim Garrison (Dordrecht/Boston/London: Kluwer Academic Publishers), 105–122; Gert J. J. Biesta, "Redefining the Subject, Redefining the Social, Reconsidering Education: George Herbert Mead's Course on Philosophy of Education at the University of Chicago," *Educational Theory* 49, no. 4 (1999): 475–492.

4. John Dewey, *Experience and Nature*, in *John Dewey: The Later Works*, vol. 1, ed. Jo Ann Boydston (Carbondale and Edwardsville: Southern Illinois University Press, 1981), 131.

5. Homi K. Bhabha, *The Location of Culture* (London/New York: Routledge, 1994), 36.

6. Bhabha, *The Location of Culture*, 177–178.

7. Bhabha, *The Location of Culture*, 228.

8. Bhabha, *The Location of Culture*, 37.

9. Bhabha, *The Location of Culture*, 36.

10. Bhabha, *The Location of Culture*, 37.

11. Bhabha, *The Location of Culture*, 38.

12. Homi K. Bhabha, "Postcolonial Authority and Postmodern Guilt," in *Nation and Narration*, ed. Homi K. Bhabha (London/New York: Routledge, 1990), 57.

LET'S TREAT AUTHORITY RELATIONALLY

Charles Bingham

Maybe the project of relational education is not viable. I say this because there are so many educational notions that will have to change in order to reconfigure education to be relational. There are so many entrenched discourses, entrenched practices, entrenched ontological suppositions, entrenched philosophies of education, all of which are highly individualistic, and the task of rethinking so much is daunting. Never mind education: People tend to think of human actions in individualistic ways in general. Making the relational project more difficult, educational practices follow the lead of this general tendency.

Some examples of individualist thinking in education are as follows: The Tyler Rationale—with its insistence on Objectives, Content, Method, and Assessment—is steeped in atomistic assumptions about students who learn curriculum as individuals. This highly influential rationale guides much of today's elementary, secondary, and higher education. Curriculum planning indebted to Tylerism treats students as disconnected individuals who are to be taught and assessed without regard to their relation to others.[1] Inspired by the efficiency of factories and mass production, curriculum planning most often sees students as units, one might even say widgets, to be educated.[2] Current political rhetoric in the United States expounding the notion that "no child will be left behind" likewise treats the single learner as a disconnected individual. According to such slogans, at-risk students will "fall through the cracks" if we let them. This image of children disconnected and falling presents a picture of the human being that is far from relational. Standardized tests, also, are clearly individualist in their orientation toward assessing each particular student. They assess the extent to which one person does or does not measure up to the rest of the lot. These normed tests measure the ability of individuals, but they do not account for the possibility that ability itself may depend on the relational context where such ability is measured.[3]

So the project of relational education might seem overwhelming. But from a different perspective, this great challenge is what makes the project appealing. Because there is so much change to be made, there is much opportunity for new scholarship and innovative practice. I think it most unlikely that any one relational idea will change all of education at once. Instead, each aspect of education needs to be rethought in its relational particulars. The particular matter of relation I will address in this essay is authority. Like so many other matters in education, authority has been understood in individualist terms. This essay will attempt to reconfigure authority in relational terms.

In order to set the stage, I begin with a story. This story was told to me by one of my students just recently, and I retell it here with great appreciation for its insight into the relational workings of educational authority, for its nuance and clarity, and for the authority that I have been granted by virtue of being able to retell it. The point of this story is to show that authority is not necessarily unidirectional, monological, or atomic. Authority might be predicated on relation.

***

Recently, a college sophomore, let's call her Julie, told the following story in class. Julie is in college to become a teacher. And, as a student who will soon be a teacher, she pays close attention to her own relationships vis-à-vis teachers so that she might learn from them habits that would benefit her own teaching. She told this story to illustrate the ways in which some university professors are sympathetic to the experiences of students while some are not.

Julie had just had a traumatic experience. Her grandmother had passed away. She had been very close to her grandmother when she was a child, though she was separated from her now by quite a distance, having moved out of state to attend college. Julie spent a week away from college to attend the funeral and to be with her family in this time of mourning. And, as it happened, she did not inform her professors about her absence until after she returned to college.

Julie was quite apprehensive before returning to her classes. She did not want to be seen as making excuses for the coursework she had missed, and she felt a bit guilty for not contacting her instructors earlier. But at the same time, she wanted to let her professors know that she had been absent for a very legitimate reason, for an event that was much more significant than any week's worth of lectures.

On the first day of her return, she approached her English professor after class. She told the professor why she had not attended the previous week's classes. The professor acted in a very sympathetic manner. She did not say a word to Julie about the absence itself, not a word about Julie's classwork. Rather, she asked if Julie had been close to her grandmother, and Julie answered yes. Julie told her of how they used to play card games together in her childhood. The professor also asked if Julie needed anything in order to get through this rough time. Julie and her English professor stood at the front of an empty classroom. "If there is anything I can do for you," the professor said, "please let me know." Julie thanked her for her kind words.

Julie contrasts this first reception to a different sort that she faced upon explaining her absence to her history professor. The history professor said, "Well, you know that you missed last week's quiz, don't you?"

"Yes," Julie responded.

"Well, you're going to have to make that up within two days."

"All right," Julie said.

"And," her professor continued, "I'll need to have a written verification of your absence. I'll need that note before you can actually take the makeup quiz. That's my policy for every student no matter how extenuating the circumstances."

Julie responded that she would provide the note. But as she recounted this story to me, she added a couple of details about what went through her mind as this incident unfolded. As Julie explains it, "As my history teacher was talking, I became so angry with her for ignoring my feelings, for being so unsympathetic. She lost all credibility in my view. After that, I refused to work hard in that class. She lost her authority as a teacher over me."

***

In this story, I am interested in Julie's comments about the way she treated the professor who was unsympathetic toward her grandmother's death. As Julie explained, her instructor's callousness caused her to discount this teacher's authority from that time forward. I am interested in this discounting because it points to a relational aspect of educational authority that is rarely investigated. Whereas educational authority is generally treated as something that one person has over another, this act of Julie's shows that she took part in a *relation* of authority. Julie's story shows that there are instances when authority works in circuits, when one person's use of authority depends on another person's participation in that authority. Julie's reaction is significant because it goes against so much educational thought. While there is much research on educational authority, authority is rarely investigated with an eye to its enactment as a relation. A slew of educational discourse assumes that authority is located solely in the hands of instructors. That is to say, it assumes that students such as Julie do not have a key role in the enactment of authority. Julie's story intimates that authority might be relational.

To highlight the uniqueness of a relational approach to authority, we can start by briefly discussing the nonrelational way that authority has been described for quite some time. Since the time of Immanuel Kant, at least, authority has been considered to be something that autonomous selves possess. For Kant, the self becomes more free, more autonomous, to the extent that one has the capacity to use the authority of one's own reason. The Enlightenment tendency to eschew the authority of the church, the state, and the medical establishment assumed that people needed to stop relying on fixed dogma. In order to be free and autonomous, in order to be "mature," one had to refuse to rely on any authority outside oneself. "It is so easy to be immature," writes Kant. "If I have a book to serve as my understanding, a pastor to serve as my conscience, a physician to determine my diet for me, and so on, I need not exert myself at all." Instead of being guided by any doctrine that resides outside of oneself, Kant stressed the following nonrelational attitude toward authority: "Have the courage to use your own understanding! That is the motto of the Enlightenment."[4] It is easy to see in this Enlightenment rhetoric a vision of authority that is still dominant today. Most often, authority is still treated as if it is something that one person has at the expense of another. To share authority, or to partake in the authority of another, is said to diminish one's autonomy, one's freedom, and one's maturity. That is, it is recommended that authority not be part of a relation. Strength is said to come from having authority to oneself rather than sharing it.

A cursory glance at current educational perspectives on authority shows a similar nonrelational perspective. For whatever reason, educational authority is often described as something that one person possesses. It is construed as an entity that, once possessed, enables one to wield a certain amount of influence over another. One often speaks of different kinds of authority—of institutional authority, the authority of the expert, the authority of one who is wise. Yet whatever its type, authority is most often treated as if it is a thing that one person or one institution has. To be sure, there are many opinions as to whether authority is useful or not. Some educators argue that it is all right to "have" authority. Others argue that "having too much" authority is dangerous for those who do not "have" it. Many educators write of ways that authority might be "shared" with one's students. But even from these different ideological perspectives, authority is considered to be something that is wielded, or shared, mainly by one person. Certainly, the common ways that we talk about authority in English tend to solidify this picture of authority as something one person possesses. Authority is often described in measurable terms: "She commands a lot of authority." People who do not "have a lot" of authority speak of the ways they might "get more." Or it is described as something that accrues: "That is the authority of age talking." Or it is said to be something that can be lost: "In front of those students, I seem to lack authority." Described as something that can be grasped and held by one person, it appears unlikely that authority might have to do with how people relate.

But how might we understand Julie's story in a different way? How might we understand it as an example of the way authority is influenced by relation? To look into this relationality, I will turn to two different theoretical perspectives, one informed by psychoanalysis and the other informed by hermeneutics. While the first perspective speaks to the ways that individuals deal with authority in relation to the details of their own life experiences, the second speaks to the ways that individuals deal with the authority of knowledge in relation to the source of that knowledge.

Relation and Psychic Life

Informed by psychoanalysis, we find that authority gets worked out in part within the inner world of human beings. It is said that the person who uses authority tends to use it in ways that reflect past dealings with authority. For example, a person might enact authority in the classroom in the same way that she is used to enacting authority as a parent, as an older sibling, or as a partner in love. A teacher who is a cruel parent at home may use classroom authority in cruel ways; a teacher who is coercive with her siblings may use authority in the same coercive way in the classroom; a dominating love partner may be dominating toward his students as well. Or a person may use authority on others in the ways that it was used on him or her by a parent, a teacher, or an older sibling. If one has been raised in an authoritarian household, one may end up being an authoritarian teacher; if one was treated harshly during childhood, one may end up using one's authority to treat other children harshly; if someone is subjected to domination in a relationship, that person may end up being dominated by students. Of course, we know that there is never a simple equivalence between past experience and present actions. It may be that one uses authority in ways that are opposite to past experience precisely because of a need to stop repeating patterns of old. In any case, a psychoanalytic perspective reminds us that the use of authority is always indebted to the psychic holdings.

And regarding the student, a psychoanalytic perspective yields the same sort of insights. Such a perspective reminds us that one tends to respond to authority in the same ways that one has responded to other authority figures in the past. How one has reacted to a parent, a sibling, or a love partner may inform the way one reacts to the teacher's authority in the classroom. For example, one might discount the authority of another person if that person were to set off authoritarian signals similar to the ones against which one had reacted in the past. If a male teacher, for example, enacts authority in the same way that one's father has enacted authority in the past, then one might discount such authority if one tended to discount the father's authority in the past. Or on the contrary, if a teacher enacts the sort of authority that the student has always respected in one's closest friends, then the student might tend to embrace that authority wholesale. However the student reacts to authority, a psychoanalytic perspective reminds us that obedience to authority rests on past experience and memory.

To return to Julie's case, it is not unreasonable that the rejection of her history professor's authority was, in fact, a rejection of the sort that she had practiced with loved ones in her past. It may be that her history teacher's stern attitude resonated in irritating ways with a stern father or mother figure, or with a callous reaction to her by a past teacher. And contrastingly, it may be the case that the embracing of her English professor's conciliatory attitude was a response similar to past responses that she had had to other figures of authority. Perhaps Julie had been used to seeking out empathetic reactions from authority figures in the past, searching for succor from kind people in positions of power. Once again, this is not to say that we know any of this speculation to be true. The point here is rather to highlight the relational possibilities of one's reaction to authority. Whether or not we know the specifics of Julie's case, it is certainly true that one's reaction to authority often has a personal history.

So far, a comparison between the Enlightenment understanding of authority and the psychoanalytic perspective goes like this: Following the Kantian tradition, using authority is a way to shore up one's autonomy and thus one's freedom. Using one's own authority keeps one from depending on the authority of others. Such use of one's authority is a conscious act, not indebted to memory or mental states. Or, if it is indebted to memory or mental states, it is so indebted only to the extent that one attempts to *shun* authority in ways that one has shunned it before. On the other hand, the psychoanalytic perspective contends that the use of authority is under the direction of past experiences that one has had with authority. The psychoanalytic perspective, as we have so far described it, indicates that *authority has us* rather than us having authority. And of the two perspectives, only the psychoanalytic offers any glimpse at the relationality of authority. Let me explain: While the Enlightenment treats authority as one's own possession, the psychoanalytic perspective reminds us that the use of authority is ultimately indebted to the extent to which the people in the authority relation are reminded of past scenarios of authority. Whether I am the one with authority or the one subjected to authority, my participation in the authority relation depends on the extent to which the other fits into my unconscious. The unconscious is

> the inner world of fantasy, wish, anxiety, and defense; of bodily symbols and images whose connections defy the ordinary rules of logic and language. In the inner world, the subject incorporates and expels, identifies with and repudiates the other, not as a real being, but as a mental object.[5]

This unconscious has a primary role in making authority into a relation. Of course, there is a major limitation to the purely psychoanalytic account that I have just described. Namely, such an account insists too much on the interior life of those who are in the authority relation. Certainly, one's use of authority is not completely dependent on one's own personal history with authority. For example, the teacher has certain real-life accoutrements of authority, without which his or her authority would misfire. In spite of one's tendency to use authority in this or that way, one must really *be* in a classroom, and one must have real students, in order to enact that authority. There are always social circumstances and real others without which, and without whom, one could not enact authority. Furthermore, only in the most uninformed of psychoanalytic thinking is one completely at the whim of past experiences when authority is enacted. A purely psychoanalytic account ignores the real-life choices made by those who are involved in the relation of authority. It ignores the social circumstances that put one in a position to enact authority, and it ignores the agency of those who use, and those who react to, authority.

In fact we should not assume that authority is completely a matter of the unconscious. If that were so, then the real other, the one who uses or is subjected to authority, would be little more than a place marker. Indeed, recent feminist psychoanalysis has insisted that there is a conscious, real side to authority. This real side Jessica Benjamin names the intersubjective zone: It is "that zone of experience in which the other is not merely the object of the ego's need/drive or cognition/perception but has a separate and equivalent center of self."[6] When one person enacts authority over another, she must deal with the fact that there are exterior elements of the other over which she has no control. Wielding authority over another is not determined solely by the distilled ways that one usually responds in an authorizing situation. The intersubjective encounter brings with it the requirement to really *be* an authority in the flesh, with all of the dominating consequences that might entail. The intersubjective bonds of authority get played out when one person interacts with an other who is not under her control, who is radically separate from herself. Whereas many bonds of authority involve internal, psychic manipulation that turns the other into an object of fantasy, the intersubjective bond requires one to deal with the other as a subject with agency.

Insofar as most prevalent accounts of educational authority are not psychoanalytic, they tend to assume that all situations of authority are intersubjective. As such, they assume that authority is primarily a battle of conscious wills. What follows from the purely intersubjective account is that enactments of authority take place as a zero-sum game in which the person in authority is bound to dominate the person on whom authority is enacted. From the student's perspective, authority depends not on past experiences, but on the force of authority that is being enacted right now. The best that can be hoped for is that the teacher will give up enough authority so that the playing field will be equal. From the teacher's perspective, the focus is likewise on the real-time application of authority rather than on patterns of authority that have been set up in advance. The teacher must choose what to do with this particular student or this particular class in the here and now, whether to give up authority, share authority, or enact it fully. From the purely intersubjective viewpoint, authority is something that the teacher wields and the student does best to avoid.

It is, I think, crucial to maintain a view of authority that deals both with the inner and the outer rather than being wed to either the Kantian account or the "pure" psychoanalytic one. It is most probable that authority actually gets enacted in ways that are both deeply personal and intersubjective. As Benjamin points out, human life takes place on the borderline between past experiences and present enactments. As such, neither the psyche nor the "real" other takes precedent over the other. Rather, memory and new experience interact; they interact in ways that allow either the success or the failure of authority.

We might reconsider Julie's example in light of both the inner and the outer aspects of authority we have examined. We might remark on the different ways that she treated her English professor and her history professor. Julie really did de-authorize her history professor. She decided, quite consciously, to write her off as an uncaring person, as a professor who no longer commanded her respect. In this way, Julie actively rejected the intersubjective experience of authority. And it might be said that she used the inner feeling of concern received from her English instructor as a fulcrum by which to expel the authority of her history professor. Indeed, she went out of her way to de-authorize her history professor. . . twice. The history professor had "lost authority" in Julie's eyes not only during the time of Julie's mourning; Julie de-authorized her professor again by restating it in my presence. The second time, like the first, it was the personal recollection of a contrasting authority figure that enabled Julie to take a stance against a "real" other. Julie twice used a juxtaposition between inner and outer in order to expel the unwanted authority of one who treated her callously. One will never know the exact set of personal experiences that led Julie to authorize and de-authorize these professors. However, it is not unreasonable to assume that the difference in reactions between the two was itself enough set up an inner need to embrace one and repudiate the other. And there was the added performance of authorization and de-authorization in front of me. I, who am Julie's teacher and therefore an authority figure over her in my own right, was called upon to acknowledge, indeed to authorize, these two reactions.

This performance of authorization and de-authorization bears on the way that the personal and the intersubjective interact with each other during the relation of authority. Julie's example is a brief illustration of the way that the inner, relational response to authority brings forth its relation into real life. While the reaction of a student to the authority of a teacher is certainly indebted to the inner needs aroused by prior experience, I want to use Julie's story as a metaphor for the intersubjective afterlife of authority. By this I mean that while the initial reaction to an authority figure may be based on past experience, there is always space for activity in the present wherein the student can actively take part in the process of either de-authorizing or authorizing. Because authorizing happens on the fault line between the psychic and the intersubjective, we must consider it to be a relational activity that begins in the psyche but ends up in the real world where humans have agency.

The Relation of Authority and Knowledge

Of course this real world is an educational world, at least as far as this particular study is concerned. This relational analysis would not have a foothold on educational authority if we did not link it to knowledge acquisition. By this I mean that if educational authority is a relation, we must also be able to discern how things get learned within this relation. Above I have addressed how authority gets either accepted or rejected in general, how one either opens the door to another's authority or closes it. When we enter an educational circuit of authority, we either want or don't want the authority of the other, it is true. But also, we either want or don't want *to know things*, to learn. How does the student partake in this learning relation? Is the student acquiescent in the face of the authority of knowledge, or does he have agency? What knowledge-related activity is carried out vis-à-vis authority? How does the student relate to authority during the learning process? Here I look to the work of Hans-Georg Gadamer.

From Gadamer's perspective, understanding entails the acceptance of knowledge from a source outside of oneself. The key term here is *acceptance*. The act of learning depends primarily on the acceptance that the knowledge of someone else deserves a spot in one's own scheme of things. When one learns from a teacher, for example, there must be either a conscious or an unconscious acknowledgment that the teacher has something to offer that is actually superior to that which one knows at present. Gadamer notes that the authority of one person over another is based

> on an act of acknowledgement and knowledge—the knowledge, namely, that the other is superior to oneself in judgment and insight and that for this reason his judgment takes precedence—i.e., it has priority over one's own.[7]

In other words, the student's role in the circuit of authority is an active one to the extent that he or she must decide to let the teacher's knowledge take priority. For authority to succeed in its aim of educating the student, the student must acknowledge that there is an important insight to be gained from the teacher. The student has the active role of authorizing the teacher by following the teacher's pedagogical lead. To learn thus entails the authorization of the teacher by the student. When the student accepts the knowledge of the teacher, she has authorized him or her.

This process of "acceptance" might sound at first glance very acquiescent on the part of the student. Indeed, it would be a thin relational understanding of authority if we were to end up by saying that the authority of knowledge acquisition is relational because the student has an active role in obeying the teacher. But as Gadamer points out, the relation of authority in education is not solely an acknowledgment of the teacher. It also entails acknowledgment of content. Yes, accepting the teacher's knowledge will mean accepting certain prejudices of the teacher, which will be limiting for the student in the sense that some of the teacher's prejudices may limit rather than enhance the student's agency. However, educational authority is also oriented around content. "This," writes Gadamer,

> is the essence of the authority claimed by the teacher, the superior, the expert. The prejudices that they implant are legitimized by the person who presents them. But in this way they become prejudices not just in favor of a person but a content.[8]

There is an acquiescence on the part of the student, in favor of the teacher. But this acquiescence is tempered by the fact that there is a content to which the student can return over and over. This content will be available in the future for interpretation and reinterpretation. Future interaction with the content will enable the student to fend off simple acceptance of the teacher that prevailed at the time of learning.

Back to Julie's case, we now leave her inner and outer responses to authority in order to focus on the educational import of her actions. The two instructors that she mentions, the English professor and the history professor, have educational roles; they are not just generic figures of authority. In fact, we have not done justice to Julie's story in an educational sense until we speak to the fact that her instructors are teachers of *something*. It is very interesting that although Julie's account of what happened to her implies the presence of both generic authority (the callous response of what could have been anyone in authority who showed no empathy toward her grief) and educational authority (the callous response of a particular instructor of history), the two very different types of authority are lumped together and treated equally. In Julie's account, she intimates that her discounting of the history professor's authority also meant that she would, in the future, refuse to take learning seriously in that instructor's class. I sense that when the history teacher "lost her authority as a teacher," what that meant, in part, was that Julie would no longer let the content of the course sink in. I picture Julie continuing on as a student in that course in a very perfunctory way, just doing enough studying to earn a good grade. To put this plainly, Julie seems to have discounted the teacher and the curriculum in one swoop.

The work of Gadamer informs Julie's story because it reminds us that authority has a textual life as well as an interpersonal one. It reminds us that educational authority can rest not only in the personality of the instructor, but also in the content that is left over after personal authority has exited the scene. In Julie's story, one senses that she discounted the knowledge that was gained from the history professor's course because of the professor's callousness. When she says that the professor has "lost her authority as a teacher over me," I can only guess that she has not taken part in the "act of acknowledgement" that Gadamer claims is so central to the process of learning under the authority of a teacher.[9] But Julie could have done otherwise. She might have acknowledged the content itself even if she chose to reject the authority of the teacher's knowledge. The knowledge-based aspect of educational authority suggests that Julie has a relation with more than the teacher; she also has a relation with the knowledge associated with that teacher. As such, she has the opportunity to return to the authority of content at a later time when the authority of the teacher is no longer at issue. In this way, the relation of authority might be measured by the book's shelf life. Indeed, in Julie's account, it seems that both instructor and content were summarily discounted. Yet in another iteration of this story, Julie might have decided to take this opportunity to valorize the authority of the text at the same time that she de-valorized the authority of the person. My point here is that we must not forget the wonderful mediating role of educational content when it comes to educational authority. Content might be seen not as that which is necessarily lost when one dismisses the authority of a teacher, but as an intermediate zone between the inner and the outer experience of the authority figure, a zone where students can have agency over the elements of authority that might remain educative in spite of a teacher's callousness.

Importantly, the content that remains after an educational relation is not subject to our inner experience of past authorities, nor does it constitute a real other. Content provides an intermediate space for experiencing a form of authority that is neither completely under our control nor completely out of our control. Indeed, texts have a life that straddles the inner and the outer. Not unlike the inner world, where, as Benjamin says, "the subject incorporates and expels, identifies with and repudiates the other, not as a real being, but as a mental object," the text has a life that one can control without the risk associated with "real" others. One can open or close a book when one wants. One can supply interpretations that are outlandishly one's own. A person can choose the extent to which she is beholden to the text without worry that the text will force itself upon her. But even better than the inner psychic world per se, the experience of reading a text also entails an interaction with something that is outside of one's self. The text, while it is under our control, is not identical to inner life.

D. W. Winnicott has said of cultural practices like reading that they provide a "third area," one that is very close to intrapsychic space but not identical with it:

> It is useful, then, to think of a third area of human living, one neither inside the individual nor outside in the world of shared reality. This intermediate living can be thought of as occupying a potential space.[10]

I would say that it is this third area that makes educational authority a particularly rich experience. Educational authority is different in kind from both the psychic version of authority offered by most psychoanalytic accounts, and from the authority that is summarily rejected by the inheritors of Kantian individualism. In fact, Kant misses something very important in his analysis of authority that thinkers like Winnicott and Gadamer, help us to recover: the cultural life of texts. When Kant claims that "I am immature" if "I have a book serve as my understanding," he misses the qualitative difference between the authority of people and the authority of books. Our responses to educational authority can use this difference to the healthy advantage of students.

And more to the point of this chapter, I would emphasize that educational is even more relational than other forms of authority to the extent that such authority resides not only on the fault line between the inner and outer, but also on the fault line between teachers and texts. Educational authority is marked by the presence of cultural texts that give the student all the more "space" for safe engagements with authority. When one experiences authority in education, one can respond to it in very personal ways, in very confrontational ways, but also in ways that rely on the staying power of content. Because the text is an alternative to the force of the other, one can respond to the other's meaning as well as to the other directly. What's more, the interplay between inner recollection, outer experience, and textual engagement provide a sort of authoritative triangulation where one can have a relation with authority in any one of a number of permutations. Unfortunately, Julie's story did not reveal the many possibilities of such triangulation, a matter to which I will soon turn.

So far, we have looked at Julie's story as a means for making the case that educational authority should be treated relationally. I have used psychoanalytic and hermeneutic perspectives to account for this relation. These perspectives shed some light on the workings of this relation. But it might be objected at this point that even if we understand the nature of the authority relation, it still remains to be seen how such an understanding can actually help us to practice education differently. It might be said that taking an X-ray of a broken bone is not equivalent to fixing the bone. Therefore, I will turn to some of the implications of a relational understanding of authority.

Once we treat authority relationally, we can encourage students to take part in education in ways that are more empowering. Let me explain. In most accounts of education, it is assumed that the teacher is the one who "has" authority and the student is the one who is passively subjected to authority. Such assumptions keep us from investigating how students might take part in the authority relation. Guided by our new treatment of authority, we might encourage students to consider how they can benefit from the authority relation by using such a relation for their own flourishing. Because students do have agency within the authority relation, it is in the student's interest to embrace authority at some times and to reject it at others. It is in the student's interest to find ways that authority can increase human capacity, and to find ways to avoid the sorts of authority that decrease capacity. It is in the student's interest to engage with authority in very personal, introspective ways at times, and to let authority figures intrude upon one's introspective space at others. Educators have a responsibility to see to it that students are not only reactive to the authority of teachers; it must be insisted that students know how to be active vis-à-vis the authority of their teachers and the authority of content.

With the relational model in mind, we might encourage students to get past current habits of accepting or rejecting authority wholesale. Most nonrelational accounts of authority leave the student with just two options: submit or don't submit. This is because authority is most often posited as something done to the student, something that can be evaded but not engaged with. Because authority has intricacies that are introspective and intersubjective, textual and personal, it is possible to encourage students to do more than reject or accept. Rather, students might be encouraged to employ and deploy, to embrace and even manipulate authority. Students might be encouraged to embrace authority at first, only to discount it later on. They might be encouraged to consider authority itself to be an integral part of one's plan of study. That is not to say that students should always be looking for ways to embrace authority, but rather for ways to engage and disengage with authority strategically.

What I am suggesting is that one's relation to authority should be an interplay between proximity and distance, between how one assimilates authority at some times and how one keeps authority at bay at others. I am suggesting that acts, like Julie's, of discounting a teacher's authority are extremely important. Julie's story shows that she took an agentive role in the authority relation. Student agency when confronted with authority figures might consist of discounting them at some times, and it might consist of honoring them at others. For example, as Julie's story seems to intimate, one can hold one authority figure at arm's length while at the same time embracing another authority figure. Just as she discounted the authority of her history professor, she was also able to embrace the more humane authority of her English professor. It is not necessary that one react to authority in general. As Julie's story has so vividly shown, one may benefit from one authority relation at the same time that one eschews another. I take Julie's embrace of her English teacher's authority to be a very important example of how students might use the relation of authority actively, how students might gain agency through a self-styled relation to authority.

Of course, what is missing from Julie's story is a nuanced consideration of the student's relation to textual authority. And as I have said, educational authority has an added relational component because of the central place of content. Thus, even as a student distances herself from the force of personal authority, it is still possible to seek proximity with the more intimate relation that one has with textual authority. In Julie's case, it is very unfortunate if, as seems to be the case, she ended up being disengaged from the subject matter of the course simply because her teacher was not empathetic. If Julie had been able to disentangle the personal from the textual, she might have been able to *split* the authority of text and person, valorizing one even while devalorizing the other. When encouraging students to engage with, rather than react to, authority, we must help them to feel empowered enough to engage with texts in spite of teachers! This may mean that students take up strategies that are at odds with the educational institution's structures of grading and assessment. It may mean that students study the content at a later time, without regard to passing a test or getting an A in the course. In Julie's case, she might have helped herself to the content offered in spite of the professor's lack of empathy, and she might have done so on her own time, even after the end of course, when doing so would not serve to authorize her teacher but would be solely for Julie's sake. Yes, we should advocate that students learn in spite of their teachers, and even in secret from their teachers. We should encourage students to be strategic enough to be against the authority of the teacher while being *for* the authority of the text.

And of course the opposite may be encouraged. There may be times when one's reading of texts needs to be augmented with the personal authority of a teacher who shakes up how we read. It may be the case that a student like Julie returns to *another* history teacher after a cooling-off period spent with the content, once she finds that the content interests her enough to seek the personal authority of one who might enable her to delve into the subject matter further. I certainly do not mean to say that empowerment vis-à-vis educational authority is always a move away from the teacher, and toward the text. Certainly, a student should also be encouraged to see the power of finding the right teacher, the teacher whose authority he or she benefits from. It seems to me that students become empowered to the extent that they entertain both the dangers and the benefits that authority figures represent. A teacher can be an aid to human flourishing, an aid to what we learn and how we learn it. Or a teacher can be as harmful as Julie's history teacher was. The point of a relational account of educational authority is to show that it is within the power of the student to discern between the authority that will lead to flourishing and the authority that will quash it. In education, such discernment must take into account the personal histories, the power-laden human interactions, and the mediating space of the text. It is the obligation of educators to help students see that authority is a relation, and that they have the power to adjust to that relation in ways that lead to flourishing.

Notes

1. See Ralph W. Tyler, *Basic Principles of Curriculum and Instruction* (Chicago: University of Chicago Press, 1969).
2. See Raymond Callahan, *Education and the Cult of Efficiency* (Chicago: University of Chicago Press, 1964).
3. The sort of relational context to which I am referring is nicely described in Barbara S. Stengel's chapter in this volume.
4. Immanuel Kant, "An Answer to the Question: 'What is Enlightenment'?" in H. Reiss ed., *Kant's Political Writings* (Cambridge, Cambridge University Press, 1970), 54.
5. Jessica Benjamin, *The Bonds of Love* (New York: Pantheon, 1988), 20–21.
6. Benjamin, *The Bonds of Love*, 30.
7. Hans-Georg Gadamer, *Truth and Method* (New York: Continuum, 1993), 279.
8. Gadamer, *Truth and Method*, 280.
9. See also Gadamer's *The Enigma of Health* in this regard, especially the chapter entitled "Authority and Critical Freedom" (Stanford, CA: Stanford University Press, 1996).
10. D. W. Winnicott, *Playing and Reality* (New York: Routledge, 1971), 110.

FROM STUDENT RESISTANCE TO EDUCATIVE ENGAGEMENT: A CASE STUDY IN BUILDING POWERFUL STUDENT-TEACHER RELATIONSHIPS

Frank Margonis

In his educational odyssey, *Sometimes a Shining Moment,* Eliot Wigginton charts the process whereby he and his students developed a uniquely powerful form of project pedagogy, and the story moves—over a period of several years—from classroom conflict to astoundingly successful teaching and learning.[1] As a rookie teacher struggling to enact a didactic classroom style, Wigginton called out resistant responses from many of his high school students. Yet his passion for the task of teaching, combined with his stubborn intolerance of poor relationships with students, moved him to seek ways of relating to his students that would meet his ethical and pedagogical expectations. Wigginton does us the service of describing pivotal moments leading to the development of this new pedagogy, and—most profoundly, for our purposes—he chronicles the different forms his relationships with students took in this process.

Once they began publishing the magazine *Foxfire,* Wigginton and his English students in Rabun Gap High School in Georgia enjoyed national attention for their widely read magazine and for the pedagogy that produced it. Drawing on the rich history of artisanship and folklore of rural Appalachia, the students researched and documented stories and crafts of local people, publishing articles, for instance, on how to build a log cabin, or on superstitions, or on famous bank robberies. The literary standards of *Foxfire* were high, and this was made possible only by an astounding level of engagement by students. Called to take on adult responsibilities and develop high-level academic skills, many of Wigginton's students responded in remarkably mature and committed ways. This collective achievement was made possible when Wigginton and the students decided to place the creation of the magazine at the heart of their English curriculum. For many educators, this was the most powerful example of the project style of teaching defended by authors such as John Dewey earlier in the twentieth century.[2]

The story Wigginton and his students tell offers us theoretical as well as pedagogical insights. In contrast to a theorist like Dewey, who focuses his attention on how students learn and the ways we can make classroom pedagogy conform to that process, Wigginton expended an extraordinary amount of his attention toward understanding the character of his relationships with students. To the authors in this volume and me, such attention to pedagogical relationships is long overdue. Many of the cases where public schools do not serve students can be productively reconsidered if we endeavor to understand why those relationships between students and teachers are failing, and if we consider examples—like the one of *Foxfire*—where potential failures were turned to successes.

In short, Wigginton helps us better understand the relational preconditions for powerful learning and teaching. His struggles to develop meaningful educational relationships with his students led him to a continual process of observation and speculation about the reasons why students act as they do. This initial concern with understanding the social dynamics of the classroom illustrates the profundity of teachers who take an ontological attitude, humbly seeing themselves and their students as part of a larger social dynamic whose patterns are difficult to disclose and whose possibilities are even more difficult to discern. Throughout the book, Wigginton tries classroom practices and observes the results; he refuses to blame the students and instead looks to the social circumstance—such as his actions, student peers' actions, and the students' relation to the subject matter—to understand why students sometimes resist and at other times respond productively. By combining Wigginton's narrative with ontological theorizing about relationships, we will argue that one can locate a dimension of classroom experiences that composes a basic prerequisite to successful classroom practice.

Wigginton's Narrative on the Transformation of Pedagogical Relationships

As Wigginton describes the social process whereby the Foxfire pedagogy was hammered out, much of his intelligence and emotional energy seems to be focused on his sometimes rocky and sometimes warm and sometimes pedagogically powerful relationships with students; it's his insightful and determined attentiveness to the relational preconditions of great learning and teaching that we will focus on here.

In the early stages of Wigginton's story, he recounts his recurring difficulties with two groups of problem students: defiant dorm students and apathetic local students. Although he clearly likes many of these kids as individuals, he is disturbed by their lack of commitment to academics and their misbehavior in the classroom. Symptomatic of the struggling student-teacher relationship, Wigginton introduces these student groups to readers using deficit terms: dorm students, who would show up at Wigginton's high school after being kicked out of several city high schools, are said to come from "unfortunate family situations" (12) that are "urban, fast-paced, and permissive" (13). Local students are said to be "ill-prepared and restless." "When in school, they seem only to know how to sneer." "The universal comment is, 'I don't care' and they really don't seem to" (25).

Wigginton's deficit descriptions of students do not, however, signal that dismal form of bad faith where teachers offer a summary assessment of students in order to justify failing them.[3] Instead, he offers us situational interpretations of the students' acts. He portrays the "resentful, rebellious, restless, angered" (82) behavior of dorm students as a response to the school's treatment of them, as an expression of "their perception that they were imprisoned in an unfair institution where every aspect of their lives was monitored" (82). Wigginton also looks to the possibilities that resistant students can—within particular situations—become motivated, engaged, and productive. For instance, he noticed during the weekends when he and some of the students would work in neighbors' yards, obstructionist behavior was transformed into cooperative work:

> [D]orm students who, on campus, were regarded by nearly all who had to work with them as rude, lazy, slovenly, devious, or rebellious (and who were often kicked out for a combination of minor offenses that usually added up to a charge of a "bad attitude"), when they were off campus in small groups doing work with me. . . were unfailingly courteous and enthusiastic and cooperative. (76)

Wigginton thus came to see his task as one of finding the social relationships that would transform student resentment and apathy into engaged learning in the classroom.

One of his early strategies of bypassing student negativity in the classroom and in his role as dorm supervisor came in the form of befriending students. By interacting informally and playfully with students, he earned their heartfelt appreciation, but he quickly found that the terms of friend relationships were unlikely to lead to powerful pedagogical exchanges. Students speak freely with a friend, and that is undoubtedly one aspect of strong pedagogical interactions, but students enjoy friendship relationships partly because they have no need to obey their friends. Notice how Wigginton characterizes his friendly interactions with students as those where both student and teacher play out the larger social dynamic called friendship: "The friendlier I was in class and in the dorm, believing that would generate cooperation, the more liberties the students took and the harder it became to accomplish anything. Both the classes and the dorm would spin crazily out of control—beyond any reach" (31). By being friendly, Wigginton called out friendly responses in students; both Wigginton and the students were falling into relational patterns offered them by the social norms of their respective groups, and all of them quickly learned that those norms did not lead to powerful learning and teaching. If the students were content with such an outcome, Wigginton was not.

Repeated breakdowns in classroom interactions led Wigginton to search for new ways of conceiving his relationships with students in the classroom. At one of the lowest emotional points, he posed the problem of their conflictual class-room to the students, sending the profound message that learning, teaching, and classroom deportment are shared responsibilities. He says he entered class and "sat down on top of my desk and crossed my legs, and said, very slowly and very quietly, 'Look this isn't working. You know it isn't and I know it isn't. Now what are we going to do together to make it through the rest of the year?'" (32). This willingness to admit vulnerability and turn to the students to address their joint problems sends a powerful signal of Wigginton's openness to student viewpoints. Wigginton also sought the students' perspectives on school and classroom pedagogy by asking for essays on students' assessments of their class-rooms. Here the open communication of friendly relationships was being turned toward pedagogical ends.

Wigginton and the students continued to analyze the weaknesses of their past practices and the potential of future practices for the remainder of that school year and in subsequent years. Wigginton asked the students to think about what an English class is needed for and what activities would best realize those needs (32). Brainstorming together, they came up with organizational breakthroughs, like the idea of having a team of class officers who would share responsibility for running the class (42–43). They also came up with significant content breakthroughs, such as the idea of running a magazine that would con-tain creative writing by high school students from the course as well as from other high schools; creative writing by professional authors; and feature articles on crafts and stories emerging from the local community (47–48). This group project guided by collective decision making created a powerful forum in which the strengths of the teacher and students—whether verbal, written, organiza-tional, or comedic, to name a few possibilities—would be able to be part of the social fabric woven in the classroom.

With these new breakthroughs, Wigginton reports that many of the stu-dents began to engage their schoolwork with a new vitality and commitment; however, many of the problem students continued to resist: one tried to burn down his podium, another drove a knife into the floor, others simply disen-gaged (55). It was at this point that Wigginton's attitude was itself transformed in relationship with one of these disgruntled pupils. When the young man informed Wigginton that he would miss the next week of school because he would be developing a ginseng bed to grow and harvest and sell the roots, Wigginton openly accepted the position of learner, asking the student to show him the process of stalking ginseng in the forest and transplanting it. The student proved to be a superb teacher, and the experience recreated the relationship Wigginton had with one of his least appreciative students. He contrasts their new relationship with the friendship relationships he had pursued earlier in his career:

> I had stumbled into a different kind of relationship of a much deeper quality. For one thing, our roles had been reversed and suddenly I was the pupil, he the teacher. I was amazed at the depth and quality of his knowledge about the woods. He knew far more on that score than I, and I could not help but respect him. He had his areas of knowledge and ignorance, and I had mine, and in that respect we were equal, each potentially able to share something with the other, to the enrichment of both. (72)

This conception of respect of different individuals' distinctive strengths appears to have characterized many of the interactions in group projects in Wigginton's English class. In learning to learn from his student, Wigginton discovered or "stumbled into" a social dynamic where sincere and profound respect can be combined with a straightforward acknowledgment of different peoples' strengths and weaknesses—equity combined with high academic standards.[4]

Perhaps it is Wigginton's growing appreciation for student competence that allowed him to turn an increasing amount of classroom authority over to students. Moreover, his relational sensibilities led him to note that—in many cases—he could call out far more profound educational endeavors on students' parts by doing less himself:

> Over time, I became more skillful at identifying those areas in any project involving students where I was taking too heavy a hand, and as I sublimated my own ego and relinquished an increasing amount of control, the involvement and cooperation of the students increased proportionately and problems with discipline virtually vanished. Some of the lessons learned on a ginseng hunt had begun to bear fruit. (94)

Once again, we find Wigginton reasoning as if he and the students were part of a larger social dynamic: By decreasing his activity he was able to increase students' engagement and initiative.

The fruits of this powerful social organization with a collective project perhaps emerge most significantly in the letters students wrote Wigginton while he was away for a year in graduate school. Having assumed primary responsibility for operating the magazine—developing new articles, soliciting articles, and handling the finances—students continually reported their achievements to Wigginton and asked for his contributions. What pleased him most about these letters is the way in which students defined themselves as a collective subject, which appeared in their letters with the disappearance of the pronoun "I" in favor of "We" (105, 115). The students, en route to creating the magazine *Foxfire*, had become a "sum greater than any of its individual parts," which happens "when students stop thinking about personal glory and strive for the success of the whole" (114). These are social relationships that support extraordinary educational achievement: Real responsibilities ensure the need to have high standards, and a respectful pattern of social engagement calls out the strengths of each student.

Thinking About Pedagogical Relationships Ontologically

In the later parts of *Sometimes a Shining Moment*, Wigginton offers generalizations intended to help us understand the success of the Foxfire pedagogy. His brief uses of pedagogical theories are devoted to showing that project-style pedagogies are in consonance with children's natural ways of learning. Whitehead, Montessori, and Dewey are invoked in spots to affirm that children assertively learn from their earliest days without schools or teachers (201–202, 208). Wigginton draws time-tested distinctions between intrinsic and extrinsic learning, and he persuasively describes the ways in which intrinsic motivation leads to much more substantive forms of understanding on students' and teachers' parts. This traditional focus on the individual learner, intrinsic motivation, and the characteristics of project-driven learning strikes me—simultaneously—as profound and problematic. These are the metaphors that allowed us to move past subject matter conceptions of curriculum and to which we owe a great debt. However, these metaphors remain individualistic, focused on the individual learner, the project, and the subject matter; as such, they leave us no way to come to grips with the intensely social nature of Wigginton's pedagogy, where the individual is not the unit of analysis, where the group is "a sum greater than any of its individual parts." Individualistic theories of learning leave untheorized one of the most provocative and path-breaking aspects of Wigginton's story: the focus on the relational preconditions of great learning and teaching.

A great many of educators' efforts succeed or fail because the relational preconditions for learning are either present or absent. Even though the forms that student resistance took in Wigginton's classroom are distinctive, student resistance in a multitude of forms is common, and such cases let us know that the relational preconditions for powerful pedagogy are not in place, that something is drastically askew.[5] The student resistance faced by Wigginton and its eventual transformation allow us a unique opportunity to think about the meaning of resistance and the possibility that conflictual student-teacher relationships might be transformed into rich and productive educational relationships. One of Wigginton's great contributions is his understanding that resistance signals the need to redevelop student-teacher relationships, and he offers us a vivid example of the radical changes that can lead to the reconstruction of student-teacher relationships.

Wigginton's narrative on pedagogical relationships may be usefully conceptualized if we turn to philosophies that have likewise emphasized human relationships. The theories of the early Heidegger and of Merleau-Ponty offer us a way of understanding the centrality of human relationships to human beings. In his reconceptualization of humans developed in *Being and Time*, Heidegger argued that our relationships to others—what he calls *Mitsein* or "being-with"—are not secondary aspects of who we are but are constitutive of ourselves from birth. Humans come to be defined as beings-in-a-situation, and our relations with the objects and people around us are considered fundamental in shaping our character; we are "always already" connected to others—both the people who are located in our local context and the people present in the languages we speak.[6] From this perspective, any learning—any relationship between an individual and subject matter—occurs within a context of human relationships.

Now Heidegger's way of speaking is not easily equated with Wigginton's language, because Heidegger's conception of being-with is ontological, meaning that he is attempting to disclose aspects of human reality, that is, aspects that characterize our social circumstances regardless of our preferences. Ontological factors set the parameters of what is possible; they constitute those aspects of a situation to which we must adapt. When Heidegger says students' characters are partly constituted by their relationships to one another and to the teacher, he is not attempting to describe a desirable state of affairs; rather, he is hoping to help us understand the social relationships that define the terms of possible pedagogical relationships. Whether we are considering the case of the student who attempted to burn Wigginton's podium or the case of students who have become a collective subject, Heidegger would direct us to ask, "What social dynamic in that classroom (including acts of other students and the teacher) made these acts of human expression possible?" Wigginton too speaks ontologically in places, such as when he says, "A remarkable thing I had observed... was how different my students often were in situations that changed the signals" (76). Here he is simply speaking about the constitution of the students' characters, and he is saying the students were different people depending on the tasks they engaged in and the relations they had with others around them.

Wigginton's central concern—namely, designing a powerful way of teaching and learning—involves a combination of ontological decisions concerning the nature of his relationships with students and ethical decisions regarding the aims he and the students hope to achieve and their judgments over whether particular pedagogical strategies do achieve those aims. Accordingly, a good many of his statements make normative judgments that a particular relational dynamic is good or bad; for instance, when he contrasts the individualistic behavior of students who strive for their "personal glory" with the collective behavior of students who "strive for the success of the whole," he clearly believes the latter is a desirable type of social relationship, and he is intimating that teachers should seek this sort of social dynamic in classes. Now, the relation of ontological to ethical statements is a matter we will address in the final section of this chapter, but we will begin with Heidegger's emphasis on understanding pedagogical relationships ontologically. The ontological attitude—whereby a teacher strives to understand the terms of his or her relationships with students as well as the possibilities for new forms of relationships—is exemplified in Wigginton's straightforward descriptions of classroom calamities and his puzzled speculations over what led students to act as they did. He assumes that his engagements with students have dynamics to which he must adjust, even if there are ways to change the dynamics themselves.

Merleau-Ponty may help us better understand Wigginton's ontological attitude, for he maintained Heidegger's ontological focus, and he extended Heidegger's conception of being-with, focusing on the experiences of interacting with others and the intersubjective understandings that are part of those experiences. Building on Nietzsche's and Heidegger's de-emphasis on the primary role of conscious understanding, Merleau-Ponty portrays a world of human activity in which human bodies relate to one another at a level of which we are not consciously aware.[7] If a teacher enters a room of warmly enthusiastic students, Merleau-Ponty's perspective would allow us to expect that the teacher's body will respond to that enthusiasm possibly with a buildup of energy and excitement; or contrarily, notice how Wigginton says his own imagination is sapped by the collective attitudes of the students:

> They enter my class, turn off their ears, turn on their mouths, and settle down for a period of socializing. Every time I think I've gotten through to some of them, one of two things happens—either someone belches and breaks the spell, or the period ends and they are out in the free world again where the last fifty minutes evaporate like mist from dry ice. They really do not see why they should have English, and in a sudden revelation several days ago I suddenly realized that I couldn't see why they should have it either . . . I keep trying to think of something that will wake them up that they may also find useful someday, and I can't. (26)

From Merleau-Ponty's perspective, we might say that the social dynamic in this classroom shapes the student expressions and the teacher's, miring all of them in an academically unproductive morass. Wigginton's lack of confidence concerning the importance of English for his students is best understood as a reflection of this social dynamic, not as a reflection of Wigginton's own character.

Whether a teacher finds her thoughts robbed of insight or whether she is enthused upon seeing her students, the teacher's conscious understanding of this social dynamic may or may not be well developed. Since our bodies enter a social dynamic of which we are dimly aware, Merleau-Ponty does not look to teachers' intentions to explain classroom dynamics. Instead, he speaks of the ways in which my acts and words are "called out" of me by the people and circumstances constituting my situation. The speaking teacher will find out what she says when she says it; just like the students, she must wait until she has acted to know what she is feeling or thinking.[8] Resistant students will find themselves acting out, and their conscious explanations for their acts may be less illuminating than explanations that tie those actions to the patterns of social engagement in the classroom. Regardless of what the students were saying to themselves as they acted out, Wigginton explains some of the student resistance by pointing to the limits of friendship as a pedagogically powerful social dynamic. In Gadamer's words, we look to see how the game plays the people, knowing that the rules constituting the game can change based on social configurations in the classroom.[9] When Wigginton and the students were playing out games of friendship, they found that it did not lead them to act in the ways that would facilitate meaningful teaching and learning, but when they developed new rules of relationships and respect, they were able to develop a game that created powerful educational interactions.

However, if we are to understand why Wigginton's students were quite content to spend class time socializing, it is insufficient to look only at the face-to-face social dynamics played out in the classroom, for those patterns are preshaped by the institutional positions of students and teachers. We cannot understand the ontology of social relationships without also considering the institutional influences that frame those relationships. A great deal of research would predict that Wigginton would face resistance from many of the working-class kids in his high school, and Wigginton also points to larger economic factors in understanding his students' attitudes.[10] In explaining why local kids really did not care about English, he says, "lots of them will never leave this area of the country except perhaps to go to war—they will never read or write—they will help with a gas station and love it—that's all they need" (26). So the economic position of students preshapes their attitude toward school, English, and Wigginton, and consequently, it makes sense to use the period in Wigginton's English class passing the time with pleasant conversation.

The institutional position of students and teachers shapes their relationships, and often the face-to-face exchanges live out those institutional determinations. The tensions Wigginton—as a middle-class urban intellectual—experienced with his rural working-class students are just one case of structural influence. When students and teachers of polarized groups meet in the class-room, both can often feel the tension, because we are partly social and historical creations of our respective groups, and many of our groups live in conflict in the larger society. It is common, for instance, for white teachers and African American students in racially polarized cities to feel tension in their classroom relationships.[11] The tension is experienced by both parties; it is in neither individual but in their relationship; and their face-to-face relationship is inhabited by the historical influences of their respective groups and their groups' relationships. When white educators meet Indigenous students in classrooms, located in towns that are racially segregated both in housing and jobs, it is as if five hundred years of colonization shapes the meaning of the relationship. Indigenous peoples' resistance to schools here has much to do with ongoing Anglo racism, Indigenous peoples' resistance to white society, and to the school as one expression of the dominant group's efforts to assimilate Indians.[12] Here, developing the relational preconditions for powerful learning is extremely difficult, and a neglect of these social realities will doom teachers and students to failure.

Wigginton shows us that the actions of teachers and students can embody and reinforce these institutional predeterminations or violate them. When, early on, he employed a teacher-directed pedagogy and adopted strict disciplinary attitudes, and when the school tightly regulated dorm students' lives, they were sending a clear message that the teachers did not trust the students. The surveillance of students' lives and classroom deportment fit well with the expectations working-class students brought to the high school, and the burning of the podium may well signal a protest against this prejudgment. Indeed, it's common for teachers to act out their structurally slotted role. For instance, several studies suggest that the most controlling pedagogies are enacted in inner-city schools where many of the students are low income and people of color.[13] Wigginton gives us an example where the teacher and students directly violated the institutional determinations shaping their classrooms. Where students expected a teacher who donned an "iron mask," Wigginton asked them what the class should do. Where students had grown to expect stern discipline and distrust, the Foxfire pedagogy gave them enormous responsibility. Where students expected school to be disconnected from their lives, the Foxfire pedagogy connected students with the rural community in ways that were both socially and intellectually engaging. This is what Wigginton referred to as creating a situation that changed the students (and we might add, the teacher as well) by changing the signals (76).

Even though the structural situation remained the same—dorm students are in the high school as a last chance and local students have no new ideas about the possibility of academic success and upward mobility—Wigginton and his students were able to develop a way of relating socially that turned academic failure into success. By analyzing their good and bad experiences in schools and by trial and error, Wigginton and the students hammered out a pedagogy that worked partly because it violated the structurally sanctioned terms of middle-class teacher/working-class student relationships. Instead of playing out the game of surveillance and resistance, the students and Wigginton created social unity with the institutional relations of the larger society serving as a backdrop.

Indeed, part of the success of the Foxfire pedagogy is that it turned to the institutional position of the students as a resource. For the apathetic local students, who comprised the largest group of Wigginton's resisters, a style of learning that brought them in touch with the elders and artisans of their region took on a religious dimension; for it taught them about their deeper connections to their group and their own historical lineage. Often unaware of the ways in which their character emerged from their groups, the students found themselves powerfully moved by the people and stories they encountered:

> Few of my students seemed to have a genuine appreciation for roots and heritage and family—the kind of appreciation that goes far deeper than simply being amazed at finding out that Grandpa can cut down a tree and make a chair or a banjo out of it or that Mom used to be a midwife and knows how to deliver babies. I'm talking about the peculiar, almost mystic kind of resonance that comes—and vibrates in one's soul like a guitar string—with an understanding of family—who I am and where I'm from and the fact that I'm part of a long continuum of hope and prayer and celebration of life that I must carry forward. (75)

Relational Ontology and Pedagogical Prescriptions

Using an ontological language, we might say that Wigginton adjusted to the social reality of his classroom when he responded to student resistance by seeking new relationships with his students. Student resistance signaled that the social relationships of his class were not capable of supporting profound educational engagement and that the students and teacher would need to find new relationships. The ontological relations in the classroom intimated that a new direction must be sought, and that the new direction would need to be one that showed students greater degrees of respect while holding them accountable for educational aims. While such ontological talk composes a small portion of statements devoted to describing what "is" the case, it nonetheless has implications for "ought" statements. The pedagogical direction chosen by Wigginton and his students was limited by the ontological situation but not determined by it; they sought a pedagogy that would fit within the parameters of the social determinants they had experienced, and as they developed new forms of relationships, they altered social reality itself.

When Wigginton and his students had experienced conflictual interactions, they had run up against structural relationships that pitted working-class students against middle-class teachers, and those tensions could not be overcome through teacher-centered instruction or by pursuing friendly relationships. When Wigginton posed the "ought" question to his class, concerning how they might all productively learn together, neither the students nor Wigginton had any easy answers. The students' initial response to Wigginton's request for a critique was silence. He says, "I realized later how helpless many of them are to come up with brilliant suggestions when, because of the way they've been taught for so many years, they can't even imagine what the options could be" (32). They spent months and subsequent years groping for suggestions of how they might carry out better relationships and better pedagogy. Having experienced the limits of their past relationships, they sought new patterns of behavior and a new language with which to prescribe their future ways of learning and teaching; in other words, they had bumped up against that which "is" the case, and they were searching for what "ought" to be the case.

Wigginton's early search for a new pedagogical approach and a new vocabulary included the solicitation of essays from students on their positive and negative experiences in schools. The comments he shares with readers touch on several themes, many of which remark on social relationships in the classroom. In many cases, the student comments begin with a description of the educational relationships they have experienced and then offer a prescription that emerges out of those experiences. Here are some examples. Is: The teacher "who will teach by not getting involved but by standing in the front of the room (apart from students and student problems) repeating over and over again his facts is nothing." Ought: "A teacher doesn't need to put on an iron mask each morning before coming to school . . . To me a teacher who is understanding and can see my problems and wants to help is the kind of person who does help" (35). Is: "My teachers never found time to help me as soon as I started failing." Ought: "I think teachers should spend time with each and every student in or out of class" (33). Is: "If the teacher is in a bad mood, then I get in a bad mood." Ought: "Teachers that take the time to realize that a student is an individual and not just one out of a group are the best teachers" (34). Is: "Last year, every time we had a test the teacher would always stand in one certain place right behind me. He would make me so nervous I could hardly take the test." Ought: "One teacher in the seventh grade stands out. She would always get all the sides to every story, and she would not let any of the other teachers say anything against the kids in her class. She would always take up for us. I never heard her say anything to a student in bad taste" (34).

These student comments offer us a glimpse of the social reality of their classrooms. If a teacher, who is pitted against her students by the institutional relationships of the larger society, seeks to cope in the classroom by putting on an iron mask and does not attend to distinctive student interests, the students—in response—do not engage with the material or teacher. The prescriptions offered by students here are minimalistic; a particular pedagogy is not prescribed, but rather a small set of ethical principles: Students want respect from their teacher; they want a classroom pedagogy relevant to their interests; and they want a teacher with enthusiasm and openness. Such principles exclude particular pedagogies, such as the callous forms of teacher-centered pedagogies criticized by the students, but they are nonetheless consistent with quite a number of possible ways of learning and teaching. When Wigginton and the students went about the task of inventing their Foxfire pedagogy, such principles established a general guide, but could not produce the pedagogy itself.

If the consideration of the dynamics of relationships guided the students and Wigginton to find their most general ethical principles, the specific pedagogical practices of the classroom were decided in a pragmatic, piecemeal fashion, with each innovation being judged by the success it brought in practice. What emerged was a form of pragmatism:

> The process of examining ourselves, English and what it's for, school and what it's for, and sampling new activities went on all year. In fact, ten years later at Rabun Gap, I and new students were still at it—still tearing things apart and putting them together in different ways. Still experimenting. Still talking. Still testing. (32)

With respectful relationships being built in the process of collective decision making, Wigginton and the students could then focus more precisely on whether a theme bulletin board controlled by the students or a magazine better suited their specific pedagogical aims. They experimented with new classroom practices, and they tested their ideas in practice. This process of envisioning practices with particular aims in mind, implementing them, and then assessing their experiences in terms of their aims was the process whereby specific pedagogical practices were determined to be valuable. Here, Dewey's description of pedagogical experimentation fits well with the methods adopted by Wigginton and the students.[14]

Establishing educationally conducive relationships among students and teachers does not, by itself, lead to the project-style pedagogy Wigginton and his students created. However, the sort of free-flowing communicative give-and-take, the willingness to try new methods and fail and return to the drawing board, and the ability to appreciate one another in the process of creating that pedagogy—these social abilities were made possible only by the relationships he and his students developed. According to Wigginton, it is this relational process that is indispensable to the success of Foxfire style teaching and learning,[15] and we might speculatively say, it's these sorts of meaningful relationships that are the preconditions for powerful learning and teaching.

Notes

1. Eliot Wigginton, *Sometimes a Shining Moment: The Foxfire Experience* (Garden City, NY: Anchor Books, 1986). References to this book will appear in the text in parentheses.

2. George Wood features Wigginton in his descriptions of progressive teachers discussed in *Schools That Work* (New York: Plume, 1992). Discussion of Wigginton's accomplishments has been understandably muted because he was eventually convicted of making unwanted sexual advances toward students, and students as well as former students testified that he had made such advances toward them. He spent a year in prison, and the judge ruled that he could not teach for twenty years (Debra Viadero, *Education Week,* November 17, 1993). Some of my colleagues have consequently refused to discuss his works, since he so clearly betrayed the trust we place in educators.

   To my mind, Wigginton's reprehensible indiscretions do not erase his educational achievements; we need all the examples of great teaching that we can muster. My glowing assessment of Wigginton's pedagogy is not intended to exonerate Wigginton but is based in the view that it's inappropriate to summarily dismiss a person by reference to his or her misdeeds.

3. Indeed, Wigginton specifically prohibits such deficit talk about students: "The best teachers never make negative assumptions about the potential of their students" (223).

4. In a later article, Wigginton writes, "Every student in the room is not only included, but needed, and in the end, each student can identify his specific stamp in the effort." "Foxfire Grows Up," *Harvard Educational Review* 1 (February 1989), 27.

5. When Wigginton lists the concerns expressed by teachers in courses on project-style teaching, first among these is, "How do I turn students around who don't care, or who think school is a waste of time?" "Foxfire Grows Up," 32. Moreover, a huge research literature discusses a dizzying variety of student resistance. Some examples include: Michelle Fine, *Framing Dropouts* (Albany: State University of New York, 1988); Peter McClaren, *Schooling as Ritual Performance* (London: Routledge and Kegan Paul, 1986); Angela McRobbie, *Feminism and Youth Culture* (Boston: Unwin Hyman); Stacey Lee, *Unraveling the "Model Minority" Stereotype* (New York: Teachers College Press, 1996).

6. Martin Heidegger, *Being and Time,* trans. John Macquarrie and Edward Robinson (New York: Harper and Row, 1962), 149–168.

7. Maurice Merleau-Ponty, "An Unpublished Text," in *The Primacy of Perception* (Evanston, IL: Northwestern University Press, 1964); Merleau-Ponty, *The Phenomenology of Perception*, trans. Colin Smith (London: Routledge and Kegan Paul, 1962), 174–199.

8. Merleau-Ponty, *The Phenomenology of Perception* 181–184, 388–392.

9. Hans-Georg Gadamer, *Truth and Method* (New York: Continuum, 1989), 93–98.

10. Paul Willis, *Learning to Labour* (Westmead: Saxon House, 1977); Jay MacLeod, *Ain't No Making It* (Boulder, CO: Westview, 1987); Jean Anyon, "Social Class and School Knowledge," *Curriculum Inquiry* 11 (1981), 3–42.

11. See, for instance, Signithia Fordham, *Blacked Out* (Chicago: University of Chicago Press, 1996).

12. Donna Deyhle, "Navajo Youth and Anglo Racism," *Harvard Educational Review* 65 (1995), 403–444.

13. Jeannie Oakes, *Multiplying Inequalities* (Santa Monica, CA: Rand Corp., 1990), 28–44.

14. John Dewey, "Education as Engineering," in *The Middle Works, 1899–1924, Volume 13* (Carbondale: Southern Illinois University, 1988).

15. Wigginton, "Foxfire Grows Up," 42.

RELATIONS ARE RATIONAL: TOWARD AN ECONOMIC ANTHROPOLOGY OF SCHOOLING

Alexander M. Sidorkin

In the industrialized world, the experience of going to school or sending one's children to school has become truly universal. Yet some very fundamental questions about this experience remain unanswered. One such question seems quite important, if only for the purposes of school improvement: Why do students do their work? What makes them come to class, bring books, fill out worksheets, listen to teachers' explanations, answer questions, take tests, and so on? I find it much easier to understand why some students refuse to do some or all of these things. From a theoretical point of view, a "normal," moderately successful, boring school is infinitely more interesting than a chronically failing school on one end, and a spectacularly successful one on the other end of the spectrum. Normality always contains a bigger mystery than abnormality, because by very definition, normality lacks prominent features and thus is more difficult to understand. We call "normal" what no longer requires and yields an explanation. Rather, we use normality as a measuring stick against which the peculiar and the unusual can be understood. One has trouble focusing on the normal, because much of our quest for knowledge is fueled by the desire to solve problems, to fix what's abnormal. Students have been going to schools for many centuries, and despite perpetual school reforming and the sense of perpetual educational crisis, most students, most of the time, manage to come to school and do their work. But why do they?

Three obvious answers come to mind first: because they enjoy it, because they understand that learning is important for their future, and because parents and other adults in positions of authority tell them to go to school and do the work. The first answer seems very reasonable, but it flies in the face of reality. Despite significant and sometimes heroic teachers' attempts to make learning interesting, schools are clearly losing to friends, television, the Internet, and computer games in terms of entertainment value they can provide. This is no accident, and not a result of a failure on the part of teachers and curriculum developers. For example, the market-driven and very creative software industry also has not been able to produce games that are both educational and entertaining. Rather, the computer games turn out to be either educational or entertaining. In most cases, learning seems to involve more work than pleasure, and by its very nature cannot be more entertaining than the entertainment proper.[1]

Let us consider the second answer. Most students have a hard time connecting each piece of schoolwork to their future until very late in high school, partly because the concept of a personal future takes time to develop, and partly because learning is broken into thousands of small increments—each individual part seemingly irrelevant to students' future lives. I can offer little theoretical argument against the second answer. Indeed, students can and should understand that every problem, every essay, every report increases their chances of future success. However, no one can demonstrate that such thinking goes on, at least until very late in high school. In real life, most students do not make the connection. Of course, every student, even a kindergartner, is generally aware of school's usefulness, but it is not clear how this general idea is linked to everyday activities of students. If school is good for everyone, why do some students in some schools seem to ignore this fact? The very fact that learning motivation varies dramatically in both intensity and character shows that schooling does not have universal appeal for most people the same way as getting and holding on to a job, for example, motivates an overwhelming majority of people. If it is true that students go to school because they need to learn, this would be the same as saying that people fall in love because humans need to reproduce. A need does not necessarily translate into a motive. For example, most people need to exercise and know about it. Moreover, many people do exercise. However, such awareness does not translate into universal or nearly universal motivation, because exercising requires sustained effort and competes with many other more pleasurable activities. Going to school, undoubtedly, is closer to exercising than to eating, sleeping, or having sex. The fact that most students are aware of potential benefits of schooling does not explain the dramatically high rates of participation in schooling.

The third answer seems more promising, and yet is unsatisfactory. If students simply obey their parents and teachers, the question remains, Why do they obey? What is the source of adult authority? Under similar circumstances, very few adults would work. Students' work is vital to all modern economies, yet students are not paid for it. Schools are compulsory but lack real means of enforcement. There are no real penalties for students who do not wish to go to school, even fewer for those who are physically present but refuse to work. How many grown-ups would work without getting paid, and without fear of punishment? Of course, parents exert various amounts of direct and indirect pressure on their children to ensure a certain level of productivity. However, for most kids, the family consequences of poor school performance are not that great. Parents are still going to provide the necessities, by law or out of parental love and sense of duty. The simple comparison between a typical workplace and school reveals no obvious reasons for students to do the work. The apparent lack of strong incentives for students makes it very easy to understand why some schools fail. It is much more difficult to say why so many schools succeed. Of course, all definitions of success are debatable. However, no one will dispute that most schools succeed in maintaining a certain level of organization, discipline, and, most importantly, a certain level of schoolwork. The question remains: Why do so many students work at school?

My interest is very far from examining learning motivation in the psychological sense, which is covered extensively in the educational psychology literature. Rather, I would like to consider it as an economic question. Schoolwork does not serve any immediate needs of the worker, and therefore does not fall into the category of immediately rewarding activities like eating, resting, or having sex. It does not usually satisfy such needs as that for entertainment or curiosity. Of course, schoolwork may entertain or fascinate, but we may safely assume that in most cases it does not. Many students do their work anyway, and this chapter is an attempt to understand why.

When individuals engage in large-scale, systematic, and prolonged activities that do not bring any immediate satisfaction, this could be considered work (labor), and an economic explanation could reasonably be expected. Many policymakers and practitioners base their understanding of schooling on a misleading macroeconomic analogy: Students (and their parents) are considered to be consumers who receive educational services from schools. Schools are public or private service providers—the analogy goes—who serve the client. No doubt, schools can be understood in such a way. However, this is not a particularly useful analogy. The truth is, most students perceive school as a chore, and rightfully so. School learning is something one has to do, like taking out trash or doing dishes or cleaning one's room. This is something they are required to do, something that eats away at free time and energy, takes years to complete, does not bring much pleasure, and consists of tasks that are almost impossible to connect to any future use. Just imagine that you would be required by law to visit your doctor regularly and undergo series of unpleasant testing procedures, supposedly for your own benefit but also to save public money. Would it still be a service or a citizen's duty? The very notion of service implies a choice to receive or not to receive it.

I have argued elsewhere that from the macroeconomic point of view, K-12 students provide many more services than they receive.[2] The schoolwork is really a chore performed by students rather than a service provided to them, because the economic benefits of students' efforts are enjoyed mostly by their future employers. Yet even if one refutes this claim, and the work of students is found to benefit them significantly in the future, one still has to describe what students do as a self-serving labor, not an act of receiving services. Simply put, students do most of the work associated with learning. They greatly outnumber teachers and administrators, while working for about the same amount of time, or even a greater number of hours per day, counting the homework. If school were a restaurant, a patron would have to bring her own groceries, rent a stove and pots, cook her own food, serve herself a dinner, and clean the dishes when done. Of course, there would be still an element of service here: The restaurant would provide supervision, advice, and assistance. However, the client would rightfully walk away with a feeling that she worked—for her own benefit and with outside assistance, but still the element of work greatly outweighs the element of service. I will assume from this point on that schoolwork is work and that schools should be considered not service-providing organizations, but places of employment for students.

Students, teachers, and administrators can be viewed as economic agents. School as an economic system organizes production, distribution, and consumption of goods and services. The most obvious observable feature of school life is organized, sustained labor performed by students and teachers. If teachers' economic motivation is relatively easy to explain, it is not the case with the students' motives. Some hidden economic mechanisms compel most students to put in long hours of schoolwork and homework. People work for a reason, and the understanding of reasons behind human work is probably the only way to attribute rationality to their work. These reasons, as we will see later, are much more complex than working for a paycheck, yet it would be implausible to assume no reason at all. An economic motive is behind student efforts, and this chapter is an attempt to discover it.

School as a Market Economy

Before we can continue, one crucial disclaimer: Schools can be viewed as small economies, but not as market economies. Can we simply apply the apparatus of economic theory to describe and explain schools? Can we think in terms of supply and demand, markets, and so on, about schools and student work? This is a tempting proposition, but it is untenable. Mainstream economic theory concentrates heavily on market economies. Most economic theory is not useable without the institution of a market and market mechanisms. Schools are not market economies, although they are surrounded by the sea of market relations, just like the sphere of domestic labor remains a sphere of largely nonmarket economy. I will try to show now that this is not a pure accident. Schools are not dinosaurs of archaic economic relations that need to be upgraded to fit the rest of the economy, as some conservative theorists argue. The attempts to understand and change schools using mainstream economic assumptions are unproductive at best, and could be disastrous at worst. There have been several attempts to understand schooling in economic terms. Such attempts have failed because of the assumed identification of economy with market economy. I will briefly consider two such attempts, one macroeconomic and one microeconomic.

Garry Becker's human capital theory is perhaps the most influential attempt to consider education in terms of market economy.[3] The theory claims that greater investment in learning leads to greater benefits for both an individual and the society as a whole. Individuals can increase their earnings if they invest in their skills. Becker provides extensive statistical data to show that higher education translates into higher earnings. The theory invoked criticism on several grounds. The return on "investment" in learning has been declining and may have been overstated in the first place.[4] Moreover, Becker seems to ignore the reproductive function of schooling. He assumes a student to be a free individual agent who chooses how much and what sort of education to obtain. This is not as much a simplification as an error, or, rather, two separate errors. First, students from low-income households, as well as many minority students, certainly do not have choice in the extent or quality of their education. This has been much argued and documented extensively in both economic theory[5] and educational theory.[6]

The second and more important error is in ascribing to a K-12 student motives that he or she generally lacks. Becker implausibly transfers market behaviors into the school environment. Behaviors of a consumer, an employee, an employer, and an investor could be directly linked to the realities of the market and described as personal rational choices in pursuit of individual interest. It is very hard, though, to imagine a thirdgrader who makes the decision to do her homework because she imagines the future economic benefits of her little investment. This simply does not happen very often, which is not to say it never happens. Although every student's behavior is guided by rational economic motives, as I will show later, such behavior cannot be described as investment. Becker's analogy breaks down on the level of a specific individual action, although the overall sum of all individual actions may look like a consequence of market behavior. Yet attributing certain characteristics to a process on the basis of its result makes for a careless theory. Just because carpet looks like grass does not mean it needs watering.

Like some of Becker's other ideas, the human capital theory is an analogy that went too far. He tries to explain a wide range of behaviors in terms of market economy: discrimination, crime and punishment, family relations, addiction, and so on.[7] These highly creative and imaginative descriptions suffer from unduly stretched analogies. It is amusing to think that criminals are rational, and that the police strive to maximize profits. It is equally amusing to think that students invest in their own skills and then cash in on higher wages. Yet it is clear that with enough imagination any behavior could be described as governed by laws of the market. Eating, sleeping, playing chess, writing books on economic theory could all be included. If market economy encompasses everything, it loses all positive content. What is next? Should one describe bird migrations or planetary motion in terms of market economy?

The most direct attempt to apply market principles to the microeconomic level of schooling is the concept of the token economy. Token economies were very popular some thirty years ago, but interest among educational researchers has been declining.[8] After initial interest in the 1950s and '60s, the token economy idea remained mostly in the field of special education, like some other behaviorist innovations. The picture is different in educational practice. I cannot find any statistics, but anecdotal evidence suggests that token programs are still used widely in many schools, especially at the elementary and junior high levels. Lack of proven effectiveness has never been an obstacle to use of an educational method. Kazdin and Bootzin wrote one of the first evaluations of this phenomenon as early as 1972.[9] Since that time, their verdict has not been significantly challenged. Twenty years later, A. Kohn essentially reiterated the same charge against the token economies: "The fact is that extrinsic motivators do not alter the attitudes that underlie our behaviors. They do not create an enduring commitment to a set of values or to learning; they merely, and temporarily, change what we do." He also wrote that "extrinsic rewards turn learning from an end into a means."[10]

Both proponents and critics of the token economy seem to believe in an utterly artificial distinction between intrinsic and extrinsic motivation. The proponents believe that schools should operate just like offices, factories, and shops. High productivity and following rules would be rewarded by tokens. The tokens, in turn, would be converted into tangible rewards. The opponents place their hopes in "intrinsic" motivation. They believe that children will somehow develop the incessant desire to add and subtract numbers, read assigned books, and memorize historical events. The whole distinction between intrinsic and extrinsic motives assumes an autonomous, isolated individual who acts without the network of social relations. An intrinsically motivated person does not care what others expect of him or her; he or she works of his or her own volition. An extrinsically motivated person is after tangible rewards; he or she also does not care about the others, only tangible rewards and punishments matter.

The economic problem with tokens is that they are not real money. For the school market economies to work, tokens have to be exchangeable for real money, and student labor would be compensated at a market-determined level. The economic value of tokens is incredibly low, considering the expenditure of labor that goes into obtaining them. Students who are forced to look at their own labor in terms of market economy quickly realize that tokens are a tremendous rip-off. My son, for example, had to read half a dozen books in elementary school in order to get a free small pizza, less than a five dollar value. Any child knows perfectly well that walking someone's dog or delivering newspapers is a much more lucrative job than the most advanced token program.

Schools and schoolwork of students just do not make much sense in terms of market economy. Student labor is not paid like almost any other form of labor in the contemporary capitalist society. Moreover, for economic reasons it is very unlikely it will ever be compensated in the same way as adult labor. Yet schools do operate, and hundreds of thousands of students perform an enormous quantity of work. Schools could be much better explained in terms of a broader understanding of economy. There is more to economy than a market.

Relational Economies

Schools have more in common with what economists used to call archaic or traditional economies. The small subfield of economic anthropology can provide a much more useful set of tools for education than the mainstream economic theory. Economic ethnography seems to take off with the influential works of economic historian Karl Polanyi,[11] although Marcel Mauss and Bronislaw Malinowski greatly contributed to Polanyi's thinking. Malinowski's study of the economy of the Trobriand Islands off the east coast of New Guinea has probably been cited more often than any other single ethnographic research in the discussions within economic anthropology.[12] Malinowski describes Kula trade as an example of an intricate economic system that involves reciprocal exchanges of goods and services without determining the exact value of each object. In fact, some objects have no use-value at all; their only value is association with former owners.[13] Polanyi convincingly shows that the concept of a market and market exchange is simply not applicable to many economies.

Polanyi critiques Adam Smith for the assumption of man's "propensity to barter, truck and exchange one thing for another." "In retrospect," writes Polanyi, "it can be said that no misreading of the past ever proved more prophetic of the future."[14] Polanyi argues that both historical and anthropological data show market economies to be an exception rather than the rule. For tens of thousands of years, individuals acted not in pursuit of their individual material interest, but on other considerations:

> The outstanding discovery of recent historical and anthropological research is that man's economy, as a rule, is submerged in his social relationships. He does not act as to safeguard his individual interest in the possession of material goods; he acts so as to safeguard his social standing, his social claims, his social assets. He values material goods only in so far as they serve his end. Neither the process of production nor that

of distribution is linked to specific economic interests attached to the possession of goods; but every single step in that process is geared to a number of social interests which eventually ensure that that the required step be taken.[15]

Polanyi develops this idea further by considering both ethnographic data and economic history. He names four principles on which an economy could be based: the market principle, reciprocity, redistribution, and householding. The market principle involves buying and selling of goods and services and is based on the interplay of supply and demand. This is what most of economic theory considers economy, and what dominates the industrialized world. The other principles have governed most human societies for most of their existence and probably still regulate most of economic activity on this planet.

Reciprocity is exchange in which the giver either does not expect anything at all in return (generalized reciprocity) or expects some return at some time in the future (balanced reciprocity). An example of the former variety in the contemporary society would be economic relations within an extended family; an example of the latter is a group of friends, who expect to help each other move and take each other to the airport or counsel each other on financial and romantic matters, but avoid keeping track of who owes whom how much in terms of the performed labor.

Redistribution involves movement of products from individual and collective producers to some center, which then redistributes the products and sends them back to localities. Redistribution occurs when a tribal leader collects food and other products from all and then redistributes them according to need, influence, and other considerations. This type of economy is only possible when most people accept the need for one person or a group to figure out the redistribution mechanisms. Not only small-scale tribal economies can be based on redistribution; ancient Egypt and the Soviet Union have created large-scale redistributive economies with entirely different technological bases. Even developed capitalist economies have large redistributive sectors in the forms of taxation and public services. There is no need to mention that the tax-based sector of economy has significantly grown since the times of Adam Smith.

The principle of householding applies to families that produce everything for their own consumption. Later, Polanyi seems to include instances of this principle into one of the others.

Economic anthropologists have done some interesting work since Polanyi,[16] and I do not intend to survey the field in this chapter. However, I find the fundamental intuition they share remarkable and very useful in educational theory. Richard Wilk has summarized it as follows: Economic anthropologists "are interested in people because they are both rational and cultural, because they pursue both money and morality."[17] A convincing answer to my question about student motivation must treat students as rational beings who will work if it makes sense for them to work. However, it would be a gross simplification to apply here the principles of economic motivation endemic to the market economies.

Instead of the somewhat pejorative term "archaic economy," I will call these nonmarket economies relational, because the key feature of such systems is that the economy is submerged, or integrated, into the larger sphere of social relations. (Marcel Mauss describes it as "total social phenomena."[18]) We can see islands of relational economies in most contemporary societies, even in the United States. There are many instances of reciprocal cooperation outside of markets. For example, most forms of friendship involve exchange of certain services. Neighbors often form de facto cooperatives that involve mutual obligations. In working-class and poor neighborhoods, people still rely on relatives, friends, and neighbors for essential services like baby-sitting, moving, car repair, security, marital counseling, entertainment, information distribution, and so on. Teenagers almost universally form groups not devoid of economic function. Members of such cliques, gangs, and loosely organized groups of friends depend on each other to provide and receive extensive educational services, psychological counseling, entertainment, and security.

In non-Western societies, even those who have superficially embraced market economic models, the sphere of relational economies may be greater in magnitude. For example, in my native Russia, mutual obligations of kinship and friendship very often outweigh purely monetary motives. What Westerners often regard as barbaric and irrational business practices often turns out to be a culturally determined blend of market and relational economies.

One common feature of relational economies is that the act of providing service to others both implies reciprocity and avoids any exact stipulations on timing or quantity of the reciprocal service. We "invest" in our friends more as an act of insurance against future unforeseen needs. I want to emphasize as strongly as I can the nonmarket orientation of the relational economies. However, one should not forget that these are still *economic* phenomena. When my family asks neighbors to take in our cat for a couple of weeks, both sides are perfectly aware of the economic condition of such an agreement. We are indebted, and there is an expectation of a returned favor. However, we are both aware of the fact that the debt may never be returned, or returned in entirely different form. When the neighbors do us a favor, we create a bond that no market theory can explain or measure, yet a bond that is as material as a signed contract.

It is not my intention to idealize the relational sphere of economy. It could be just as exploitative and manipulative as the market sphere. It certainly cannot replace the market, on which we rely for most essential goods and services. The market is remarkably efficient and flexible in organizing large portions of contemporary society. However, it is not the only and not the universal economic mechanism. Moreover, a society totally devoid of relational economy is hardly an ideal. I want to establish two facts: that relational economies still exist, and that their mechanisms are very different from market economies.

School Economies

Economically speaking, American schools are much closer to tribes of the Pacific than to corporations located nearby. Their economic relations are embedded in other social relations. For a variety of reasons, schools cannot and should not develop into true market economies, which does not mean that they cannot improve the types of economies they do have.

One important feature of school economies is that they do not provide means of physical survival. This is not an exceptional feature, of course, because the classic case of Kula trade also involves exchange that is not essential to survival, yet is central to the cultural life of the islanders. A reasonably well-organized school provides rich social experiences to students in such a way that it becomes essential for their individual well-being—not in the sense of preparing for the future, but as here-and-now well-being.

A successful school is an economic system where schoolwork is an integral part of social relations, and the bulk of social relations is integrated into the functioning of school as an organization. In other words, the secret of the remarkable performance of an average school is in its ability to link social and cultural practices of children and adolescents with the formal practices of teaching, learning, and administration. As with any economic relations, students here have a direct interest in remaining at school and in maintaining a certain level of social order there. In the crudest terms, students exchange their labor of schoolwork for the opportunity to build social relations with peers and adults. The successful school is one where teachers have insinuated themselves into the social network of children's and adolescent society. Kids will do the chore of schoolwork if and only if they receive something in return. This is a common principle of all economic behaviors; there is no reason why it should not apply to schools.

How exactly does the nonmarket economy function in schools? I suspect the bonds of mutual obligations involving schoolwork are created in great many ways. For simplicity, let us consider the general principles outlined by Polanyi. Teachers and school administrators use both reciprocity and redistribution principles. Reciprocity is most commonly used in a single classroom; the mechanism of redistribution is more prevalent at the level of the school. Let me give some examples to illustrate how these two principles may be used.

Reciprocity is more often used in direct relationships between a teacher and a student. Most teachers realize that the formal teacher authority is not nearly enough to maintain order in the classroom, let alone to ensure even a moderate level of learning. Teachers thus engage in an ancient game of mutual favors: They do favors for students, which students implicitly agree to repay with good behavior and reasonable effort in schoolwork. The services teachers provide can be very diverse; they depend on what students may want and what a teacher can offer. Sometimes students just want personal attention, sometimes some tokens of respect and affection. Little kids want hugs; older kids need a sympathetic ear; everyone needs recognition.[19] They might be interested in what teachers know and what teachers can do. Teachers lend them influence, connections, advice, or recognition. Teachers can give them praise, candy, stickers, and good grades (yes, tokens built into the fabric of social relations may actually be perceived as signs of genuine respect, not unlike bracelets and necklaces of the Kula trade). Teachers can teach them how to play a new game or tell them something new about their athlete hero. Teachers may have information they need, or they can keep secrets. In short, a child and adolescent may want a million small and big things from an adult. The trick is not so much to figure out what they want and what teachers have, but to initiate the exchange on terms of generalized or balanced reciprocity rather than one-to-one discrete trade. In other words, having the merchandise does not automatically guarantee a deal. Not unlike adult relational economies, the economy of school relation will work only when it is well oiled with personal trust and legitimized through tradition.

The principle of redistribution comes into play when educators capitalize on their central position within the school's social organization. An example of the redistributive economic relationship in school is a school dance. Students may want to attend the dance for their own reasons, which may have nothing to do with adults. Nevertheless, they recognize the need for organization, space, security, finance, and so on. In other words, in order to obtain the good of attending a dance, they need the mediating and regulating role of the school's adult authorities. Everyone contributes to the success of the dance. In a certain sense, students exchange services, but adults are needed to regulate the exchange. Again, teachers and administrators need to insinuate themselves personally into the event of the dance so that the mediating services they provide will be associated with specific persons rather than with a faceless institution. Such an association creates the relationship of mutual obligation, which can be later turned into good behavior and schoolwork efforts. Students contribute their labor of school learning to teachers much like ancient Egyptians used to build tombs for their pharaohs. The pyramids were not built by slaves, but were rather a result of labor tribute/tax paid to the pharaoh by free peasants. It was a pragmatically senseless but economically necessary part of the society. The pharaohs needed the godlike authority to distribute food and goods effectively. Students will invest in collective teacher authority only if the authority will be used to stimulate effective exchange of services among students. Students will pay their labor tax to the cast of benevolent rulers (teachers and administrators) if and only if they understand the real or perceived benefits the cast provides to them. Of course, this logic applies not only to dances, but also to other events of school life, such as homecoming rituals, proms, and so on.

Student labor can be considered within an economic framework Rhoda Halperin calls administrative production. She describes a village of Chan Kom in the Yucatan peninsula, where "every male was required to perform *fagina* labor as a public service without remuneration." Performance of this service was required to maintain residence and status, including the right to communal land. This is another form of labor taxation, a form of communal labor that defines participants' role in the community. Halperin cites an earlier study of the village that noticed, "the most public spirited do more than others." She comments: "The measure of 'public spiritedness' was directly proportional to a citizen's tolerance for servility, and willingness to perform fagina became a litmus test indicating loyalty to the *comissario*, who functions as a patron to his loyal village clients."[20] Of course, *comissarios* regulated *fagina* and ultimately found a way of using it for their own benefit. The whole relationship is based on the monopoly on land, which allowed the elites to control labor.

Students' work in schools is not unlike administratively regulated communal labor. Each student is obliged to work several hours each day, and the measure of his or her dedication is proportional not only to the loyalty to adult authorities, but also to the school community. A combination of purely administrative sanctions (such as detentions, reprimand, etc.) and an ideological pressure ("stay in school" propaganda) is used to secure an acceptable level of labor. Yet, as in the Mexican village described by Halperin, in the American school the success of the communal labor depends on whether the educators have found a way of controlling the resource of social life schools provide. Obviously, in small rural communities, schools control much of social interaction among students. The schools there effectively control the cultural life of the community through athletic events and much of other entertainment output. In addition, schools can control parents relatively easily by the threat of creating a negative image of the family should students refuse to cooperate. The same mechanism cannot work in an urban setting, simply because schools do not control as much of the social resources. Students have plenty of opportunities to socialize outside of school; parents' communities are fragmented and not dependent on schools to maintain social status. Quite often, a racial and class divide separates teachers from students and parents, which makes loyalty to school authorities socially unacceptable. In such circumstances, student work becomes closer to forced labor than to the patriarchal communal labor such as *fagina*.

Consider a school that many would call failing. The classes are unruly, student and teacher absenteeism is high. No one seems to be learning; teachers spend their time establishing a semblance of order in classrooms. The school principal spends most of her time doing "crowd control." Police officers have an office on the premises. From the point of view of economic anthropology, this may be a case of failing relational economy. For most students, doing schoolwork and following the rules do not bring any status gains or recognition from the people they care about the most—their peers. In order to maintain memberships in peer groups, students need to sabotage the schoolwork and school rules.

School Reform Program

The implications of the economic anthropology of schooling can be significant, and their full exploration falls outside of the scope of this chapter. One implication is that both in the theory and the practice of education, adults must learn to treat students as rational beings who will work when it makes sense to work. At the same time, what makes sense to a laborer in a market economy may not necessarily be applicable to a student who works in a nonmarket, non-cash economy of schools.

Another implication is critical toward current efforts in educational reforming. The authors and proponents of accountability reforms would like to increase productivity of student labor. If the functioning of schools depends on the sort of relational economies I have described, accountability pressures may have a destructive rather than constructive impact on the nations' schools. Attempts to intensify both student and teacher labor through accountability measures may lead to more instability within relational school economies. The accountability pressure undermines the traditional side of relational economies. The communal labor is regulated by traditionally accepted levels; and increase is always resisted and resented—not because of the absolute growth of work time, but because it contradicts the logic of communal labor. If relational economies are eroded and destroyed, systems run by direct threat of force will replace them, the sort of schools with full-time armed police officers, metal detectors, random locker searches, and so on. In economic terms, this would be a slide from communal labor to forced labor, from a village to a prison camp.

Another mistake is to include schools into macroeconomic relations through various voucher initiatives. This logic implies that if schools begin to compete, they will create a market of educational services. Not a totally unrealistic expectation, but it will of course dramatically increase the inequality of education. This criticism has already been developed, and I do not wish to repeat it. However, the voucher solution completely ignores the question in the beginning of this chapter. Why would students want to do their work once their parents chose the school? How would the act of choice automatically translate into an economic force that motivates students to work? In other words, it is unclear how a competition among schools will change student motivation one way or the other.

An economic anthropology of schooling can help develop a meaningful alternative reform program for public schools. A school improvement informed by the economic-anthropological perspective would seek to strengthen the relational economies of schools. One assumption of such a program is that schoolwork is a form of labor, and as such needs serious incentives. Learning in schools is only a part of a much more complicated web of social relationships, and it cannot be treated as an isolated activity. Learning may not be changed or improved without improving the workings of the entire relational economy of a school. Hence, reformers need to design certain institutional changes that would allow educators to offer more services to students and be more effective in their mediating roles. The value of peer culture and peer interaction should be recognized, and systematic efforts must be made to integrate it with the sphere of academic labor. Teachers cannot be expected to simply create good personal relationships with their students out of nothing. Schools need to provide many opportunities for teachers to interact with students outside of traditional classroom settings. The reform needs to counteract the tendency to cut down the nonacademic time in the school day. Rather, the nonacademic time should be much better organized, and much better funded. The idea that the roles of a teacher, of a social worker, of a school counselor, and of a neighborhood club organizer should belong to different people has to be reconsidered. While market economies always benefit from division of labor, in the nonmarket relational economies the opposite is true. Only combining several functions in the person of a teacher can assure that teachers can both receive and dispense services. Of course, such a reform program requires an acknowledgment that the aims of education go well beyond the preparation of a skilled workforce.

Notes

1. Alexander Sidorkin, "Labor of Learning," *Educational Theory* 51, no. 1, (Winter 2001), 91–108.
2. Sidorkin, "Labor of Learning."

3. Garry Becker, *Human Capital*, 3rd ed. (Chicago: University of Chicago Press, 1993).
4. D. W. Livingstone, "Beyond Human Capital Theory: The Underemployment Problem" <http://www.oise.utoronto.ca/~dlivingstone/beyondhc/>.
5. S. Bowles and H. Gintis, *Schooling in Capitalist America: Educational Reform and the Contradictions of Economic Life* (New York: Basic Books, 1976).
6. Michael Apple, *Cultural and Economic Reproduction in Education: Essays on Class, Ideology, and the State* (London: Routledge, 1982). Henry Giroux, *Education Still under Siege* (Westport, CT: Greenwood, 1993).
7. See, for example, a collection by Becker's students and followers: Mariano Tomasi and Kathrin Ierulli, eds., *The New Economics of Human Behavior* (Cambridge and New York: Cambridge University Press, 1995).
8. ERIC database produces 28 entries for "Token Economy" published between 1995 and 2002, down from 57 published between 1985 and 1991, and 79 between 1975 and 1981.
9. A. E. Kazdin and R. R. Bootzin, "The Token Economy: An Evaluative Review," *Journal of Applied Behavior Analysis* 5 (1972): 343–372.
10. A. Kohn, "Rewards versus Learning: A Response to Paul Chance," *Phi Delta Kappan*, 74 (1993): 784–785.
11. Karl Polanyi, *Primitive, Archaic, and Modern Economies* (Garden City, NY: Anchor Books, 1968).
12. Bronislaw Malinowski. *Argonauts of the Western Pacific: An Account of Native Enterprise and Adventure in the Archipelagoes of Melanesian New Guinea* (London: G. Routledge, 1922).
13. Karl Polanyi, *Primitive, Archaic, and Modern Economies*, 200.
14. Karl Polanyi, *The Great Transformation: The Political and Economic Origins of Our Time* (Boston: Beacon Press, 1957), 43.
15. Polanyi, 46.
16. See, for example, Susana Narotzky, *New Directions in Economic Anthropology* (London: Pluto Press, 1997).
17. Richard R. Wilk, *Economies and Cultures: Foundations of Economic Anthropology* (Boulder, CO: Westview Press, 1996), xi.
18. Marcel Mauss, *The Gift: Forms and Functions of Exchange in Archaic Societies* (Glencoe, IL: Free Press, 1954).
19. See Charles Bingham, *Schools of Recognition: Identity Politics and Classroom Practices* (Lanham, MD: Rowman and Littlefield, 2001).
20. Rhoda Halperin, *Economies Across Cultures: Toward a Comparative Science of the Economy* (New York: St. Martin's Press, 1988), 120.

PART 2

DEMOCRACY, CARE, AND STRANGERS: CHALLENGES TO RELATIONS

DEMOCRACY NEEDS STRANGERS, AND WE ARE THEM

Jaylynne N. Hutchinson

A question that has long intrigued me as I have studied in the fields of multiculturalism, philosophy, and the democratic community is how strangers who create a nation can form relations that will allow them to (1) retain a unique sense of their identity (cultural, ethnic or otherwise), (2) develop some sense of commonality without erasing unique identities, and (3) strengthen a commitment to be active participatory citizens in a democratic community. Our nation has grudgingly emerged from the hegemonic sleep of the "melting pot" theory where one must give up one's identity in order to fit into a common culture. Following on the heels of the civil rights movement and with the advent of the politics of identity, folks began (self-consciously and with self-determination) to identify who they were as individuals, but more significantly for the polity, who they were as groups or communities of people. Hence, the various people's movements in the '60s and '70s defined themselves and no longer allowed themselves to be identified by the dominant culture.

Even within the politics of identity movement, further self-definition emerged. This was clearly (but not painlessly) seen as a necessity in the women's movement, for example, which was primarily defined by white middle- to upper-class women. Women of color and women from working classes raised their voices and questioned whether or not "feminism" as defined by the first wave of feminists really included the life experiences of women of color or the working-class women. Of course it did not, and so riding the incoming tide of identity politics, further self-definition occurred.

Disturbed by the fragmentation that began to appear as groups and then groups within groups began to self-identify and collect themselves in a space where each could set the agenda, the communitarian movement began to raise questions of what would bring us together as a community.[1] Some critiqued the communitarians for seeking a "common culture" that was only a chimera in the first place.[2] Others critiqued them for creating exclusionary communities defined again by those of the dominant culture (even if they were more liberal!). Communitarianism is a movement with no place beyond already self-identified communities. It is a movement that may help people who choose to share themes or values or projects in common, but it does not help us move closer to living together with difference. Because we have been unable to develop a flourishing democracy, Judith Green describes the implications when she states that this failure to develop a flourishing democracy "manifests itself in a generalized insecurity, a shared loss of the sense of agency that once allowed diverse people to believe that they could participate in shaping the public terms of social life, a shared lack of meaningfulness in daily activities, and a widespread loss of permanence in life commitments that leads many people to focus on pleasure-seeking and pain-killing, rather than risk a more complex kind of pursuit of happiness."[3]

While many dedicated activists continued to work tirelessly in their communities through all these political movements and academic debates, only a few in the scholarly community have attempted to put forward a new way of understanding how we can substantively overcome the fragmentation of the politics of identity without reverting to the hegemony of the myth of the Common Culture. One of these scholars is Iris Marion Young, who has drawn on Sartre's notion of seriality to explain how we can retain the unique identities that define who we are, but not fall into the myth that we all share common commitments and goals, or that we must.[4] Such work begins to point us in the direction of remaining strangers. This is an important starting point and must be understood and have attention paid to it in order for strangers to invigorate a democracy rather than fragment it.

While I find myself excited about the ideas Young proposes, I fear she does not go far enough to overcome the dilemma so that her concept of seriality could encompass a notion of praxis—that is, how can we apply the theory to our actual experiences of living in the world so that lived experience can inform our own theory and constructs of meaning? While it may seem counterintuitive, a strong, flourishing democracy requires strangers, but not just any relation of strangers will be fruitful. Hence, we must explore a pedagogy for strangers that will sustain a democracy.

The type of democracy that we hope to sustain is one that Judith Green has called "deep democracy." Green describes it thus:

> Deep democracy would equip people to expect, to understand, and to value diversity and change while preserving and projecting both democratically humane cultural values and interactively sustainable environmental values in a dynamic, responsive way. Existentially, deep democracy would reconnect people in satisfying ways, thus healing our currently dangerous pathologies of existential nihilism and ontological rootlessness. It would direct and support collaborative local communities in reconstructing civic institutions, processes, and expectations. Deep democracy is both the goal and the process that can facilitate the emergence of "publics" that can exert effective transformative influence within our democratically deficient world societies.[5]

Still, we have not discovered the role of the stranger within this rich notion of democracy. Young argues that we form identity groups around fluid and changing situational contexts. She rejects essentialism, both for the individual, and also for a group or culture. This is where she draws on Sartre's seriality and gives us examples, such as a group of people waiting for a bus that is late. All these people have a common goal (to travel somewhere), and many have time constraints that make the tardiness of the bus problematic. A group or community or serial of people is beginning to form around the circumstances in which these folks find themselves. In like manner and in a more serious vein, Young argues that women as a group do not share an essentialist nature, nor are all women oppressed in the same way. But women can create a serial grouping or community when they do find themselves in a similar context or situation.[6] In a large nation-state, it is not possible to create a list of common specific commitments acceptable to all people at all times or an essential nature of what it means to be an "American." Therefore, if we are to move beyond fragmentation of self-identification without returning to an assimilationist model, we must understand a different way to see each other as strangers.

While Young alludes to it when she draws on Sartre's concept of seriality, she does not take these contexts seriously enough to acknowledge the significant identity-shaping role that seriality, or some form thereof, plays in the creation of human beings and in a democracy. Of course, the occasional experience with the tardy bus will not be a significant factor in creating who we are as individuals. But it does make us different people depending on whether we grow up in a bustling metropolis utilizing public transportation or on a rural farm where the amount of rainfall, for example, has significant meaning for your means of making a living. And more significantly, while I agree that women do not share an essential nature, there are enough similarities in the patriarchal context in which girls and women exist that our very identities are formed and shaped by this serial relationship. It is not one that can be left behind as soon as "the bus comes," for example.

The role of the stranger in a large democracy where anonymity is a given is crucial. A flourishing democracy relies on a particular relation of narrative life experiences that exist between strangers. To illustrate and punctuate the abstract concepts of my argument, I will utilize examples of lived experience that will shed light on the value of strangers remaining strangers, yet in a distinctly unique relationship. (Utilizing these examples is a methodology on which I rely that I refer to as narrative inquiry.) Before turning to the narratives, let us briefly examine potential roles for the stranger in a democracy. Remember that all of these roles represent potentialities only. There is no guarantee that having strangers in the midst will bring about any of these roles (and attendant insights). That is where the Pedagogy of Democratic Narrative Relation comes in. But more about that later.

Strangers teach us to respect those different from ourselves, especially when we live and school and work in fairly homogeneous and/or segregated communities. With a pedagogy, we can broaden our perspectives by understanding the stranger that we are, as well as the stranger that others are in relation to us.

Strangers help us define ourselves. I am not you and you are not me and that is okay. The paradox of this situation is that we really are intertwined even through this relationship. The stranger creates a boundary, and a boundary is always a part of us. With a pedagogy, we can develop our identities with much more depth and breadth. By seeing the "other," we are presented with alternative ways of being in the world. While the vast majority of us will most likely remain in the paths by which we have been socialized, some of us will step outside those boundaries as we see what others present as possibilities.

Strangers are a part of the reality of living in a large nation, and this reality is growing ever more real and costly as technology provides immediate access to others around the globe, not just within our own nation. Given how many folks we know in the world, we truly are a planet of strangers. A pedagogy can make this reality meaningful.

Strangers in a democracy ask us to defend one another's differences, even if we disagree with them. This is no small task, even though we at times do this well and at other times we fail. Lives literally depend on our ability to understand this. Hence, a pedagogy will teach us to live together as many strangers, to be different and to be at peace.

The discussion of the role of strangers must be followed by an in-depth look at how education and schooling in the United States can apply the concept of a Pedagogy of Democratic Narrative Relation in order to go beyond the minimal (and sometimes dangerous) notion of tolerance in a democracy and move toward a realization of a type of intimacy among strangers that will allow a democracy to exist in a meaningful and productive way. Education can provide opportunities for all involved with schools to develop the habits of democratic hearts and minds so that we can look forward in peace, especially living among strangers.

A major goal of this book is to make relations visible in a variety of ways. I have chosen to focus on the relation of strangers. Strangers help define us. At first glance one may think this is done through a "this, not that" framework. But at times the more subtle "this, *and* that" framework provides more insight into who we are. This may seem at once contradictory. How can one have a relation with people who will be forever strangers? To help answer this question, let's look at how community is currently conceived. Generally there are three types of community. First, community is created through familial and friendship ties. Usually we understand friendship relationships to be positive aspects of our lives. We hope that familial relationships can be positive as well, and in many cases they are. But we would be remiss if we were not to acknowledge that for many folks, family has also been a cause of pain and frustration. Even so, these familial relationships, whether they be experienced in a positive or negative light by the individuals involved, always bind us together. Though we may be grown adults ourselves, we often still hear the "voice" of a parent echoing as we move throughout our lives. We will be forever bound in a relationship with family and friends.

Most people may think of the second form of community—that which is created when people with similar interests come together. We have multiple examples of this in our nation, ranging from sports to music to political causes to gardening and cooking clubs. This community is created when one is a participant, such as a soccer player or a musician in a string quartet. A more diffuse type of community may be formed by those who identify as fans or as appreciators of the particular interest. For example, one may not play a musical instrument at all, but consider oneself a fan of jazz and be an aficionado with great knowledge of the topic and pure enjoyment. And certainly we have seen fans of sports teams who themselves do not touch a ball but will "bleed" the colors of their team! These are all types of communities that contribute to who we are. In studying southern and northern Italy Robert Putnam reports that the stronger these local interest-based affiliations are, the stronger the sense of democracy in a nation.[7]

Schools represent this kind of community. While the shared interest that brings people together for school may not be that of the child or young person attending third grade or eleventh grade, it does represent the interest of a community, a nation, and significantly, the interest of parents. Hence in most cases, each academic year we have children, some of whom have never met, come together with a teacher, who is also often a stranger, for the purpose of teaching and learning. In best-case scenarios, educators work throughout the year to develop and sustain a sense of community in their classrooms and schools. Unfortunately, in too many schools, kids and teachers remain strangers while involved in a common interest.

The third type of community is one that is minimal and is the type of community that some folks want! This is represented by the political thought of classical liberalism and one of its political counterparts, libertarianism. Rather than focus on libertarianism (other than to say that those who hold this view seek only the most minimal aspects of community connection on a political level), I would like to focus on the more common principles of classical liberalism that represent the dominant political system in the United States today. The community that is created by this political system is one wherein principles of classical liberalism infuse most all the institutions of our dominant culture and hence are part of the socialization of those who reside in this nation. These principles include (but are not limited to) a focus on individual identity and individual rights, freedom, autonomy, a common civic culture, and an equal respect and regard for the equality of persons, particularly as recognized under the law. Classical liberalism also relies on concepts of neutrality and objectivity in implementing these ideals. In a more colloquial sense, hard work, fairness, earning one's way in life, pulling oneself up by one's bootstraps, all represent aspects of an ideology embedded in our institutions through which we pass as we grow up in this nation.

Some would say that this is enough of a framework to bind our democratic nation together in community. In *Liberal Virtues*, Stephen Macedo argues that classical liberalism is strong enough to hold together a prosperous democracy.[8] I suggest that we must seek something beyond this and that there can be, indeed there must be, a pedagogy of relation wherein strangers remain strangers. Classical liberalism does not talk about the necessity for such a pedagogy, but simply assumes that the participants in such a democracy will be of equal value and worth and will each contribute to the well-being of such a polity. Macedo argues that if problems arise, a neutral and objective judicial and legislative system will mediate differences and problems among citizens.[9] Such assumptions are far too broad and misguided.

Yet one may claim that a relation of strangers is a paradox. This is true. In one sense such a relation is obviously abstract. It is about holding a relationship with anonymous others (otherwise they would not be strangers!), but at the same time it is particular and concrete because the others are real people, some near and some far. One of the important aspects of understanding democracy is that it is full of paradoxes and is not defined as simply as the Enlightenment model of classical liberalism would have us believe. That is fine. Democracy is messy.

One of the most likely critiques of my notion of a relation of strangers at this point is that I am creating something out of nothing . . . "straw concept" perhaps. This critique points out that while I may call this a "relation of strangers," if people remain as strangers, there simply is no relationship regardless of what I claim. In other words, one can't be a stranger and not a stranger at the same time. This defies logic, but as I indicated earlier, democracy is full of paradoxes. Here is where I must put forward my best case for why there is a substantive relationship of strangers that is crucial to a democracy and that our social world would benefit by understanding how a Pedagogy of Democratic Narrative Relation would strengthen this relationship. In addition, if this relationship and its attendant pedagogy is ignored, our democracy will be substantively weakened.

Experience, Imagination, and Possibility

To illustrate the claims I am making, I will draw on stories of relation with strangers through narrative. It is important to say at this point that I am not assuming that everyone has had the experiences I describe in the following. But the value of narrative is in seeking the themes that grow out of the narrative story and then determining and imagining how the themes illuminate the ideas and how many of us, while not having the exact same experience, will be able to identify with the narrative thematic that is developed. Taking narrative stories that one person tells and expanding these stories and making connections with other experiences in our own lives "allows us to particularize, to see and hear things in their concreteness."[10]

This is one place where the need for imagination is crucial and has long been a binding glue in social worlds that flourish. As Maxine Greene states, "the role of imagination is not to resolve, not to point the way, not to improve. It is to awaken, to disclose the ordinarily unseen, unheard, and unexpected."[11] The power of this in a democracy is that it allows growth. As a society, we are still working on how we can live in peace given our democracy of multiple lived experiences. Greene acknowledges this struggle and the attendant role of imagination and narrative when she states,

> It took time before we became acquainted with—and were able to accept—the enormous variety of human lives, the multiplicity of faiths and ways of believing, and the amazing diversity of customs in the world. To come to terms with such additional realities always involves a risk, one many adults are still unwilling to take and to see their children take. If those children do have the imagination to adjust to what they gradually find out about the intersubjective world as they move further and further from the views of their original home, they are bound to reinterpret their early experiences, perhaps to see the course of their lives as carrying out the possible (among numerous possibilities) rather than the necessary.[12]

While the stories are too numerous to share, as I have reflected on my comings and goings amid a world of strangers and being a stranger myself, I have chosen two in order to illustrate this work.

Illuminating Glimpses: Trick or Treating

As a youngster growing up in the Pacific Northwest, I loved Halloween. This strange attraction has continued into adulthood, and as I have reflected on why this might be, I have found connections with my topic here. Halloween night was one of the few nights as children that we could run free. In many ways, it seemed free from the constraints of the adult world. Certainly, the myths of the "netherworld" were set free and our imaginations roamed. As dusk moved into darkness, the October neighborhoods were filled with the spindly fingers of the bare-branched autumn trees that were silhouetted against the moonlit evening. The giant fir trees would sway in the fall winds and bend this way and that, looking like shadows of ghosts and ghouls. In our neighborhood there were no sidewalks, but groups of children would scurry from home to home, romping over lawns and piles of autumn leaves. More than half of the excitement was seeing the witch, the ghost, the Dracula rush by on the other side of the road...all dangling bags of candy. In this earlier day, there were few parents who were out and could interrupt our imaginary world.

As my grade school pals and I walked up the steps to the nearest house, we would appreciate the glowing faces of the jack-o'-lanterns on the porch. Depending on how scary the house was, we would carefully ring the doorbell or knock. As the door opened and we chorused, "Trick or treat!" we had a peek into the world of strangers whom we did not know. On these dark October nights, when the doors opened and glowed with light, we had one of the only chances ever of looking into how people in our community lived. While I never thought of it at the time, upon reflection, what we found was comforting. As we peeked around the tall legs of the adults or waited until someone came back with a tray of goodies, we usually saw or heard a TV going on in the background...and perhaps saw the living room with a couch and lamps and a chair or two. In fact, while each home was very different in style, they each had an entryway, perhaps stairs, a living room, smells of cooking, and sounds that were familiar. We were connected that one night a year by the glimpse into the homes behind the doors we knocked on, doors that otherwise remained closed and forever shut to us. The darkness of the evening gave stark contrast when the door opened for just a short peek into the lives of strangers, and the boundary between strangers and intimates blurred for a second or two.

We already had preconceived ideas of many of the houses from our walks home from school. One house belonged to the "mean ole lady" and another was the one with the "dog that bites" and another housed that neighborhood "crazy guy" in our young minds. But in the rush for Halloween candy, not a door was missed. By opening the door just a crack on Halloween night, each of the homes so labeled during the year allowed us to see that they were really not too different from us. But after that night of trick or treating, the labels would go back and we would steer clear of the requisite houses, but with a slightly modified and mediated understanding. Trick or treating was a night ripe with the relation of strangers. At no other time would people open their homes to all these parentless children of the community. This one night a year, our community connected through ways that went far beyond candy.

Hugging Strangers: Baseball in Seattle

The year was 1995. They said baseball would never succeed in Seattle. While the city had had a major league franchise for years prior to that, they rarely won, they played in an ugly covered dome made of concrete and astroturf, and attendance was sparse. But as some folks know, Seattle had drafted a future Hall-of-Famer, Ken Griffey Jr. The team was being built around his talents. As the team began to win, more and more fair-weather fans began to return to the games, and in 1995, the Seattle Mariners major league baseball team made a run at the playoffs. My younger son and I attended a couple of games during the season, but the game that caught my eye and gave me pause to reflect on strangers was the one that culminated in the division championship tiebreaker against the New York Yankees. We found our seats fairly high up in the rafters. I was hoping no one would squeeze in beside us, but of course, a game of such magnitude was sold out, and coming toward us were two older fellows with what I deemed were funny and raggedy T-shirts and scraggly hair, with beers and banners in hand. As they squeezed next to us, I rolled my eyes at my son. Here we were, he an appropriately dressed "preppie" at the time, and myself, of course, a proper college professor who enjoyed the fine points of the game!

In recounting this story, I hope my judgmentalism is coming through. Clearly I felt that, somehow, we were more "refined" than these two men sitting on either side of us. I will spare you the play-by-play call of the game, but it was one of the most exciting sporting events I have ever attended. It was won by the Mariners on the last play of the game by Griffey Jr., who electrified the crowd by racing from first to home on a base hit to score the winning run. The crowd went wild, the team went wild, the sound was deafening, and the next thing I knew, I (my dignified self) was on my feet jumping up and down and screaming like every other fan. The man sitting next to me was up waving his banners and yelling as well. After hugging and high-fiving my son, without even a second thought, I turned, and the weird guy sitting next to me and I were hugging too. I was hugging a complete stranger (and I come from stoic Scandinavians who rarely hug anyone)! But it didn't matter. We were sharing in the moment . . . two complete strangers from very different backgrounds who came together for a moment in time and who would never see each other again. We were strangers, but in a unique way, we were intimates because of the lived experience we had just shared. Even today when Seattlites get together and talk about baseball, the talk will turn to that final game in 1995 and whether one was there or not.

I realize that not everyone will relate to my Halloween or sports tales, but each of us has stories of brief interactions with strangers. These stories represent our linkages and relation with strangers that give vitality to a democracy. John Dewey indicates in *The Public and Its Problems* that we must revitalize our face-to-face local communities, "understood as diverse lives interconnected and sustained by full and free communication, because this is the birthing place of the democratic desire, the testing place for social inquiry, and the launching place for a broader, translocally dispersed 'Public.'"[13] We need these multiple ways in which we can gain glimpses into other's lives and they into ours; we need opportunities where we can each be outsider-insiders at times. The more such encounters we have, the more we are deepening our relationships with the abstract and the concrete stranger. As we do this, the more likely we will be less afraid, judgmental, or dismissive.

Unfortunately, as we lose more and more public spaces where strangers come together, we are losing opportunities for this interface between strangers. It would be less than responsible to ignore the changing nature of our society and send our children out without parental supervision on Halloween night, for example. But if we are losing spaces where we have such encounters with strangers, we need to replace them with others that are responsibly safe.

Invisible and Locked within Our Heads

Was it the famous Pogo who told us, "We have seen the enemy and it is us"? Twist that saying a bit and we have, "We have met the stranger and it is us." We are always strangers, and at the same time, always intimates. The human ego-centric self does not always see this. We are too often locked away in our own heads, living only in the world of familiar relationships. Hence, it is important to examine how we ignore the relation of strangers, or said another way, how this relation remains invisible to us although it should be explicit. I will discuss three ways this occurs.

One way we ignore this relationship is through *commodification*. In our contemporary world almost everything has been given a market value, including relationships. We are led to think that this car, cologne, or pair of jeans will get us the relationship we desire. We are led to believe that we can buy our way into a relation and that we can be part of the "right" group, that is, the group with which we want to identify. And unfortunately, too often we judge others by those same market-induced relationships. We may stereotype people who drive BMWs or, conversely, old and rusty cars. We may think one way about the young man who wears Abercrombie & Fitch and Gap clothing with a Stanford ball cap, and another way about the young man who wears FUBU baggy jeans and a hooded jacket. These market-driven values actually create, or should I say miscreate, relationships between strangers.

A second method through which we ignore the relation of stranger, is when we are involved in *chimerical relations*. In other words, we are in an unreal relationship. What might this be? Since the advent of television, we have spent less time together as citizens and neighbors and more time watching TV as a means of relaxing after work. With the mobility of society, extended families in less physical contact with one another, and increased commute time to work, less time is left for face-to-face contact with others. Over the last fifteen years we have created relationships with and around common television shows, for instance. The characters in *M*A*S*H** or *Seinfeld* provided water cooler or lunchroom talk at work. It was as if they were our friends. Today it may be *Friends* or the new breed of reality shows. These television characters represent the familiar and common experience we have. Yet it is simplistically obvious that we have no relationship with the characters in these shows, and it is complicatedly interesting that we could build up relationships with others about them.

A third method through which we ignore the relation of strangers is in our refusal to look at the present *beyond our personal "shores."* A compelling example of this is illustrated by Michael Apple and James Beane in *Democratic Schools.*[14] They speak of an elementary class that took time for current events coverage each week. One week they discussed the "natural disaster" that struck a Central American nation. High amounts of rainfall had caused a mountainside to give way and destroy homes, injure many residents, and even kill a large number of people who had made their home there. This was named a "natural disaster." But Apple and Beane ask us to consider whether or not it truly was a natural disaster. Surely the rain was a natural occurrence. And surely the losses of lives and homes were disasters. But they argue that there was nothing about the disaster that made it natural. Rather, the way we in the United States and the media *named* this event made us think it was simply one of those tragic things. It turns out that no one who lived in the fertile valley was harmed, because in this particular nation, only the poorest of the poor are pushed to the unstable mountainsides to live. This means that the disaster was a social, political, cultural, and economic one. It was not natural. But as long as we see it as natural, we will not take steps to change the conditions that caused it because those conditions remain hidden by the language we choose to label it.

In like manner, these past years have brought demonstrations in some of our cities regarding the globalization of world markets. Students in some schools have learned about the sweatshop labor conditions behind a number of our most highly regarded American trademark products. U.S. citizens are traditionally a compassionate people, so why is it that we go on buying the products whose manufacturing outside our country harms children, women, and men?

While particular corporations make enormous profits from our purchases and the cheap labor overseas, little information is given to us as citizens in our schools or through our media that would help us act toward a stranger in a compassionate way. We either don't know the information or we choose not to know so that we don't have to act. This is not the type of stranger relation that will sustain a democracy. In fact, it will slowly erode it.

Ethic of Care for Social Justice

One way to address this problem is to recast the ethic of care as the ethic of care *for social justice*. By definition, a democracy offers ideals of social justice to all citizens. Social justice requires a motivation to act, and motivation to act requires emotion. Feminist theorists have articulated the need to recognize the role of emotion in the creation of knowledge and the moral domain. Educational theorists have also articulated the need to recognize the role of emotion in learning. This is one significant reason why the classical liberalism paradigm is not robust enough to help a large democracy flourish. In its quest for the ever-unattainable position of neutrality and objectivity, classical liberalism eschews emotion. It is seen in opposition to rationality and reason. Others have argued that even reason encompasses emotion. Either way, it is clear that education in a democracy requires an acknowledgment of and engagement with emotion.

In *The Invisible Heart: Economics and Family Values,* Nancy Folbre lays out her argument that economists have not taken seriously the role of care in social well-being.[15] While modern economists define our economy and democracy through the use of Adam Smith's "invisible hand" paradigm of achievement that guides the market, Folbre states that the "invisible heart" of care has been ignored. There has been an assumption that somehow there will be an ever-present sense of care. This is simply another example of the invisibility of women's work in society for hundreds of years. In our changing world, where more and more women are in the workforce and girls and young women grow up with the opportunities to pursue virtually any career, who has stopped to ask, how will the nature of nurture continue?

In this way, the three Cs of care, concern, and connection that Jane Roland Martin espouses in *The Schoolhome* move from being misunderstood as a throwback to some nostalgic sense of family, to a vigorous way to approach our world through education.[16] Instead, the three Cs should be viewed as generating some of the toughest educational questions we can ask of our students: *Why should we care? How can we demonstrate our concern? What is our connection?* Take these questions and apply them to issues of sweatshop labor and instead of ignoring the topic, one asks: Why should I *care* that a child ten years of age works twelve-hour shifts in intolerable factory conditions? How can I, as a student, demonstrate that I am *concerned* about these labor practices (perhaps boycott, demonstrate, write letters to the corporation)? And what is the *connection* between my going to see a multimillionaire ballplayer and the company whose product he endorses paying unlivable wages to its overseas workers? For all intents and purposes, the people most negatively impacted by my purchase of a product so made will always remain strangers to me. But I *am* in relation with them. We cannot be afraid to tap into the human emotion to which the three Cs call us.

A Pedagogy of Democratic Narrative Relation

The kinds of questions posed above will be encompassed in a Pedagogy of Democratic Narrative Relation for strangers and will bring us closer to a concept of "deep democracy" that Judith Green describes. In *The Power of Their Ideas: Lessons for America from a Small School in Harlem*, Deborah Meier shares with us the set of questions that their faculty developed that permeate their pedagogy, curriculum, and school. They are:

1. How do you know what you know? *(evidence)*
2. From whose viewpoint is this being presented? *(perspective)*
3. How is this event or work connected to others? *(connection)*
4. What if things were different? *(supposition)*
5. Why is this important? *(relevance)* Or simply said, who cares?[17]

Asking these five questions, or those associated with Martin's three Cs or some iteration thereof, is the basis of a Pedagogy of Democratic Narrative Relation. Greene states that a "formal education that does *not* prepare students to be participants in and builders of deep democracy is an education that *perpetuates the unsatisfactory status quo*—and also deprives students of *the stimulation of the real, the knowledge of the different,* and *the richness of subject matter for lifelong reflection* that the world's diverse cultural traditions have brought into being."[18] Hence, if we do nothing to change the pedagogy of relation in schools, we will be perpetuating the status quo.

So what's education to do? What pedagogy enhances such a relationship with strangers so that democracy can flourish? Currently there is a disjuncture between the schools we have, where we try to create a known set of relationships, and the community that follows as students enter a larger world of strangers. What do we do to prepare them for such a shift?

We must create many opportunities for us to peek into each other's lives without interfering with them. This is far different than the noninterference role that civil libertarians or even classical liberalism would seek. Rather, this view acknowledges how important it is to know of and about the differences among us, to have some shared communities, but also to feel deeply respectful of and acknowledge the necessity for others to be separate and self-determining. We must create publics—spaces where people who are basically strangers have opportunities to come together to experience. We sit side by side at a musical festival, at an outdoor community movie. We have no intention of moving from strangers to friends (although this may happen on occasion with some folks we meet). We need to take our students into the public, and if there are not public spaces, perhaps we could create them with our students (a garden, a ball field, a theater).

This is not necessarily an easy task. For example, there are times when we may not be a part of the lives of people for whom we care or with whom we share common commitments. There are some Native American ceremonies that are not open to the nonindigenous people of the United States. In the same way, as a faculty member I may work in solidarity with faculty from dominated cultures but not be invited when they hold their own meetings. As a person of the dominant culture, I must respect that difference and not feel slighted. It is a respect for their self-determination, and applied more broadly, it is a respect for the role of the stranger in society. It is not only teachers and students who need to work in this capacity of moving outward to create publics. It is up to community groups and organizations to create publics as well. The cost of symphony or theatre tickets, for example, is exorbitant. These organizations, with adequate support, should have community outreach and be involved in a combination of bringing their performances to various communities and making it possible for students and their parents to come into performances in their own spaces. Here is where we need to step back from the intensity of commodification and provide opportunities for those who do not have the luxury to choose between rent and a concert ticket, medicine or the theatre. This is where the strangers must stand in relation to one another and create a public space to be.

We know we live among strangers, and it is when individuals or groups of individuals begin to hate, discriminate, create obstacles, and endorse or participate in violence that we must act. But rather than asking the simplistic question, "Why can't we all just get along?" we need to create a sense of acceptance, trust, and deep respect for the stranger or for those with whom we are not in contact. How can we do that? In *Feeling Power*, Megan Boler is worried about the lack of moral action and commitment that passive empathy engenders.[19] Boler warns against presenting the "other" in a superficial and ahistorical manner that might be done by well-meaning multiculturalists. There must be a different format where we can come to know the stranger without infringing on the stranger who does not seek for us to be a part of his or her life or community. As Charles Taylor has argued, we must understand the "horizons of significance" that frame who we are and who others are and how we have become.[20] These horizons include the depth of historical movements and paradigms, the roles of religion and spirituality, family, culture, and even the parameters of our physiology. How much are these topics, taught and learned with depth and breadth rather than with mere memorization of isolated facts, a part of our school systems?

In order to reach the depth and breadth necessary for the Pedagogy of Democratic Narrative Relation, we need to understand that emotions are a vital part of our students' education. When we fall back on pseudoneutrality and objectivity alone, "just the facts, ma'am, and nothing but the facts," then we are not educating for a world of strangers. Understanding the role of strangers in our democracy requires that we *feel* that role and the connections, as discussed in the questions that educators should be helping their students to ask.

Last but not least, we must create the opportunities for students to be rubbing shoulders with strangers. Don't mistake my intention here—we don't have to be buddies with everyone! We can remain strangers. Sometimes these learning relationships will unfold and flower into communities or personal relationships, but it is more than okay for our students to spend a little time looking into and experiencing the lives of others and then walk away. Returning to their communities of learning, they can then delve into the meaning of those experiences. Often we paint too rosy a picture for our students if we are educators who have a commitment to social justice. We lead our students to believe that we can change the world too easily, that we can love everyone and respect all and get everyone to agree (with us). This is such an unrealistic expectation that it will always fail in the lives of our students, and when these undertakings fail and we are no longer with our students to help them process that, they often give up and go back to living the lives of the status quo. Better to help them understand their relationship with strangers in their midst and strangers across the globe.

The implications and consequences of a Pedagogy of Democratic Narrative Relation will include the following critical tasks:

— Learn enough about each other without ironing out all the uniqueness of our differences and be comfortable with remaining strangers.

— Understand that strangers do not pose a threat to us individually or as a group. We can allow and should even welcome a variety of languages, customs, dress, and faiths in our society.

— Be especially aware of the long-dominated cultures in the United States. As we have heard, we are a nation of immigrants. But it is critical that we ask why so many of European background have blended into the U.S. culture and why many in the Native American, African American, Latino, and

Asian American cultures still struggle with receiving all the promises of democracy.

— Recognize that we do share similar human needs across the many cultures in our society, but we must be sure that we unlock our heads and not expect every culture to express or meet those needs in the same way as we do. We have to give up the (sometimes conscious, sometimes unconscious) notion that people who are different than we are want to be like us.

Greene reminds us that "our discussions of standards and curriculum frameworks and outcomes still have not touched seriously upon the matter of our purposes as a society; upon what it means to educate live persons, to empower the young not simply to make a living and contribute to the nation's economic welfare but to live and, along with others, remake their own worlds."[21] To do so will require many communities of the type we are most familiar with, but in addition, a deep democracy, one that offers opportunities for all to flourish, will require and appreciate strangers. Thank goodness we are them!

Notes

1. See Alasdair MacIntyre, *After Virtue* (Notre Dame, IN: University of Notre Dame Press, 1981) and Amitai Etzioni, *The Spirit of Community: Rights, Responsibilities, and the Communitarian Agenda* (New York: Crown Publishers, 1993).

2. See Michael Sandel, *Liberalism and the Limits of Justice* (Cambridge: Cambridge University Press, 1982) and Will Kymlicka, *Liberalism, Community and Culture* (Oxford: Clarendon Press, 1991), especially Chapter Four.

3. Judith Green, *Deep Democracy: Community, Diversity, and Transformation* (Lanham, MD: Rowman & Littlefield Publishers, Inc., 1999), vii.

4. See Iris Marion Young, *Intersecting Voices: Dilemmas of Gender, Political Philosophy, and Policy* (Princeton, NJ: Princeton University Press, 1997).

5. Green, *Deep Democracy*, xiv.

6. Young, *Intersecting Voices*, Chapter One, 12–37.

7. Robert Putnam, *Making Democracy Work: Civic Traditions in Modern Italy* (Princeton, NJ: Princeton University Press, 1993).

8. Stephen Macedo, *Liberal Virtues: Citizenship, Virtue and Community in Liberal Constitutionalism* (New York: Oxford University Press, 1990).

9. Macedo, *Liberal Virtues*, 47.

10. Maxine Greene, *Releasing the Imagination: Essays on Education, the Arts, and Social Change* (San Francisco: Jossey-Bass, 1995), 29.

11. Greene, *Releasing the Imagination*, 28.

12. Greene, *Releasing the Imagination*, 21.

13. John Dewey, *The Public and Its Problems* (New York: Henry Holt, 1927), quoted in Green, *Deep Democracy*, 47.

14. Michael Apple and James Beane, eds., *Democratic Schools* (Alexandria, VA: Association for Supervision and Curriculum Development, 1995), 14.

15. Nancy Folbre, *The Invisible Heart: Economics and Family Values* (New York: The New Press, 2001).

16. Jane Roland Martin, *The Schoolhome: Rethinking Schools for Changing Families* (Cambridge, MA: Harvard University Press, 1992).

17. Deborah Meier, *The Power of Their Ideas: Lessons for America from a Small School in Harlem* (Boston: Beacon Press, 1995), 50.

18. Greene, *Releasing the Imagination*, 67.

19. Megan Boler, *Feeling Power: Emotions and Education* (New York: Routledge, 1999).

20. Charles Taylor, *The Ethics of Authenticity* (Cambridge, MA: Harvard University Press, 1991).

21. Greene, *Releasing the Imagination,* 170.

BETWEEN STRANGERS AND SOUL MATES: CARE AND MORAL DIALOGUE

Bonnie Lyon McDaniel

Not long ago I listened to a story on NPR about a program in Seattle designed to create stronger bonds between students and their school community. The program, Project SOAR, began twenty years ago to help teachers and elementary school students develop social skills that would allow them to form stronger relationships with each other. Researchers who kept track of the students through middle school and high school found that the students who participated in Project SOAR were significantly less likely to drop out of school, abuse drugs, or engage in delinquent behavior as teenagers.[1] Project SOAR's goal of creating caring communities resonates with feminist educators' call to create caring relationships at school. Around the time Project SOAR was getting started, feminist philosopher Jane Roland Martin argued in her book *Reclaiming a Conversation: The Ideal of the Educated Woman* that cultivating students' capacity to care and relate to others should be a central aim of education. There appears to be a growing consensus across different disciplinary boundaries that students in America are too isolated from the other human beings they encounter at school, and that schools should be places that facilitate learning through caring connection.

I am deeply sympathetic with this overarching educational goal, though I suggest that educators in favor of creating caring relationships at school proceed with caution. We should be thinking not only about the potential gains of such a change; we should be thinking about the possibility that we might lose something of value in the transformation as well. Can relationships be harmful as well as nurturing? If so, how can we distinguish between the relationships we want and those we do not want as we advocate building caring communities at school? Is it possible to have too much of a good thing when it comes to strengthening bonds among members of the school community? Perhaps looser bonds at school leave more space for individuals to critically reflect on their conventional beliefs relatively free from the sort of pressure to conform that might overwhelm students in a tightly bonded school community. In a democracy, we want our schools to create citizens capable of critical reflection as well as to create persons who manage to make it to adulthood without succumbing to the risks of adolescence.

In this chapter, I will explore the possibility that strengthening social relationships at school interferes in some way with the goal of creating democratic citizens. Eamonn Callan articulates this concern particularly clearly in his book *Creating Citizens*. Careful consideration of his argument leads us to think harder about how relationships work. What sort of relationship facilitates the expression of difference, and what sort of relationship stifles such expression? Here a foray into psychoanalytic theory offers us a model of a good-enough relationship—one that creates room for individuals to express their unique subjectivity while preserving the relationship. I believe that the construct of the good-enough relationship may be particularly useful for those interested in creating classroom relationships that facilitate dialogue across gender and race differences.

First, let us explore the possibility that caring relationships might detract from the civic education we should want for our students in a democracy. Callan's concern is that adopting an ethic of care in the classroom undermines serious moral dialogue. Equating care with conviviality, Callan claims that by prioritizing caring relationships in the classroom, teachers tempt students to transform the real moral differences that exist between them into matters of mere taste in the interest of maintaining interpersonal harmony.[2] Caring relationships may facilitate communication between soul mates in private life, so the argument goes, but in the public spaces where democratic citizens meet, such relationships are more likely to cloud discussion. It is better, Callan contends, to conceptualize citizens' moral dialogue as occurring among detached strangers, rather than soul mates.

Let us consider more closely Callan's claim that the prioritization of relationship between participants in a moral dialogue jeopardizes an individual's serious moral commitments. What is the nature of the commitments that would be endangered by caring relationships? In Callan's formulation, a critical commitment is one that is internalized so that it comes to be part of the structure of the self. In contrast, a commitment is merely volitional if it is a preference that one happens to have but that one may lose or gain without making one's life morally better or worse.[3] Attending critical moral commitments, Callan claims, are moral emotions: One feels moral distress when one finds that one's commitments are not upheld, either in oneself or in others. Indeed, the experience of distress in the presence of moral failure is part of what it means to have a serious moral commitment. Because this is true, Callan is concerned that privileging an ethic of care in the classroom would make it difficult for individuals to express the authentic emotion of distress that sometimes accompanies one's serious moral commitments. He reasons that if our care for one another is the most important aspect of our conversation, then we are likely to suppress feelings of moral distress in the interest of maintaining interpersonal good will. Rather than endanger the relationship by expressing a potentially distancing emotion, we are tempted to "recast real moral conflict, with all its attendant distress and estrangement, into some more comfortable mode of divergent valuation."[4]

In the interest of preserving the authority of truth, Callan concludes that an ethic of care is not particularly useful as a guiding ideal in moral dialogue under conditions of moral pluralism. Callan understands care to involve intimacy, which means a desire to share intense experiences with another. It is simply not feasible, he concludes, to expect to sustain intimacy among interlocutors in moral dialogue in a society in which individuals have different, and sometimes conflicting, conceptions of the good. Under conditions of moral pluralism, Callan contends, dialogue between individuals with divergent moral commitments is best conceptualized as a conversation among strangers, rather than soul mates.

Let us consider Callan's formulation in a concrete context that might arise in a classroom. Imagine two students, John and Amy, who have very different moral commitments when it comes to the issue of affirmative action. Now imagine that John and Amy find themselves in a classroom in which an ethic of care prevails. John and Amy, along with the rest of the class, will be encouraged to develop caring relationships with each other. When they discover their divergent beliefs about affirmative action, they face a dilemma. Because both consider their beliefs about affirmative action to involve serious moral commitments, they feel moral distress when they encounter each other. What Callan seems to be concerned about is that, instead of expressing moral distress and risking the possible estrangement that might come from it, John and Amy will convert their serious moral difference into a simple matter of differing opinions in order to preserve the bond of solidarity that has been cultivated between them in their caring classroom. Instead of seeing themselves as individuals who are defined by their moral principles, which includes their positions on affirmative action, they begin to see themselves primarily as partners in a caring relationship, with different, but nonthreatening, tastes when it comes to music, fashion, and moral beliefs. To avoid the outcome of fostering intimacy in public places at the expense of truth-telling in moral dialogue, the integrity of individuals' moral commitments is best protected and preserved by imagining moral dialogue in the classroom as occurring between strangers.

Callan has hit upon a genuine difficulty in the conduct of moral dialogue. Our care for one another sometimes does take the form of a desire for intimacy and accord with others, and some forms of intimacy may very well be threatened by presence of moral difference. But must we think of care as a form of intimacy that always seeks union or oneness with the other? We have not necessarily demonstrated the poverty of understanding ourselves to be in relation with one another as we seek the truth in moral dialogue just because we have pointed out that care as a form of intimacy that seeks accord with others is likely to impede serious moral dialogue. We need to think more carefully about relational forms that lie in between the poles of detached strangers and fused soul mates. Are there other ways to conceptualize forms of being in relation that are conducive to truth-seeking through dialogue in public settings?

Here a few concepts borrowed from the psychoanalytic theory of D. W. Winnicott can help us make distinctions between relational forms that seek union and are threatened by expressions of difference, and those that can endure expressions of difference and even thrive on them. The concept of the good-enough relationship was originally developed by Winnicott to describe a relational pattern between mother and child conducive to the development of the child's capacity for living authentically and creatively. In infancy, Winnicott claims, the child experiences the mother responding nearly perfectly to her instinctual needs. This near-perfect response permits the child to develop the illusion of omnipotence, which as Winnicott describes it, is "the illusion that there is an external reality that corresponds to the infant's own capacity to create."[5] It is the parent's job to gradually disillusion the child of the fantasy of omnipotence, which can be accomplished successfully within the context of a good-enough relationship. As the parent's response to the child's needs gradually becomes less than perfect, the child inevitably feels frustration. The relational pattern that takes shape between the two as the parent responds to the child's frustration has important implications for the child's subsequent development.

Extending Winnicott's relational model in her book *The Bonds of Love,* Jessica Benjamin claims that the good-enough response from the parent will fall between the extremes of permissiveness and retaliation. In the permissive response, the parent cannot endure the child's anger and seeks to maintain accord with the child by satisfying his desires as perfectly as possible. This response keeps the child locked in the illusion of omnipotence: The self-sacrificing mother is experienced merely as an extension of self, and the child feels as though he has no separate agency of his own. As Benjamin describes it, "the child experiences his expanding elation, grandiosity and self-absorption as flying off into space—he finds no limits, no otherness. The world now seems empty of all human life, there is no one to connect with, 'the world is all me.'"[6] Although the child can make the cognitive distinction between self and other, on an emotional level the other is experienced as appendage or mirror of one's self.

In the retaliatory response, the parent makes it clear that the child's anger is not acceptable. The child's will is overpowered by the more dominant will of the adult. In order to stay in relationship with her parent, the child learns that her own will must be sacrificed. The retaliatory parental response also leaves in place the child's fantasy of omnipotence, but in this case, omnipotence is projected onto the all-powerful parent the child then seeks to please. This child too can learn to make the intellectual distinction between self and other, but the child's felt sense of self is "false." As Benjamin describes it, "The false self is the compliant, adaptive self that has staved off chaos by accepting the other's direction and control, that has maintained connection to the object by renouncing exploration, aggression, and separateness."[7] It is worth noting that in both the retaliatory and the permissive relational response, a type of unity or accord between parent and child is preserved, but this unity is detrimental to the child's process of differentiation and the development of his relational capabilities.

In the good-enough relationship, the parent neither withdraws nor retaliates in the face of the child's anger, but survives it. The child's anger is recognized, but placed within boundaries. The parent who survives the child's act of destruction in fantasy becomes, in a sense, unhinged from the child's fantasy of him or her. Because the parent does not act according to the child's fantasy role by "disappearing" in response to the act of destruction, nor by retaliating with an equal and opposite act of destruction, she is experienced as lying outside of the borders of the child's fantasy. As Winnicott tells us, it is of developmental importance for the child to experience his anger in this way, for if the child feels as though he has destroyed "everyone and everything, and yet the people around him remain calm and unhurt, this ability greatly strengthens his ability to see that what he feels to be true is not necessarily real."[8] In the good-enough relationship, the child comes to experience the mother as a separate locus of subjectivity with desires, beliefs, and projects of her own.

What are the implications of the concept of the good-enough relationship for our thinking about the ways in which relationships might impede or facilitate truth-telling in moral dialogue? Winnicott's model begins with the assumption that fantasy plays an ineradicable role in our mental lives. Because this is true, human beings throughout their lives have difficulty experiencing others as separate centers of subjectivity. If a child's early relationships are good-enough, she learns to distinguish her fantasy of the other from the real, external other. As she matures, she gains the capacity to bring moments of mutual recognition (in which she feels for the other as a separate center of subjectivity) into tension with her fantasy of the other (as the one who can meet her needs perfectly). When she goes to school, she will be better equipped to sustain good-enough relationships with members of her school community: Though she may still desire to have her own views mirrored by others, she is able to keep this desire in balance with the desire to recognize and relate to the other who exists outside the bounds of her fantasy. If her relationships are good-enough, she will be able to experience the discomfort that arises as serious moral differences are ex-

pressed without immediately capitulating to the superior will of the other or attempting to convert the other to her point of view. The good-enough relationship provides space for two subjectivities to engage in serious moral dialogue.

For this relational accomplishment to occur, two things must happen. First,
the real difference that the other makes must come into view for the subject. In
the mother-child dyad, this means that the mother must be willing and able to
assert her own interests in her relationship with the child, while at the same
time recognizing the child's acts of self-assertion. Second, both parties must
remain in the relationship. The discovery of the other's survival (in the wake of
an attack on the level of fantasy) leads to the possibility of relating to the other
as an external center of subjectivity only if an emotional resonance is maintained with the other. In what follows, I briefly explore the possibility that pervasive forms of social inequality may make the achievement of relations of
mutuality even more difficult. If this is true, then truth-telling in moral dialogue,
particularly among members of privileged and less privileged groups, may be
facilitated if students are able to enter into good-enough relationships with each
other.

Jessica Benjamin claims that common cultural representations of gender
make it less likely that individuals will develop the capacity to recognize the
separate subjectivity of others. In societies that associate masculinity with power
and agency and femininity with passivity or self-denial, real men and women are
likely to take on aspects of these roles, consciously or unconsciously, and try to
live up to the idealized images of masculinity or femininity implied by them. For
example, women who have internalized the ideal of the self-sacrificing mother
may have a difficult time insisting on the value of their own interests when
these conflict with the interests of their children. Benjamin describes how cultural representations of gender can affect the dynamics of real mother-child relationships, leading to a persistent cultural pattern in which the subjectivity of
the mother is denied:

> The negation of the mother's independent subjectivity in social and cultural life makes
> it harder for her to survive her child's psychic destruction and become real to him.
> Since the child has not been able to engage in successful destruction, he is less able to
> distinguish the real person from the fantasy. The larger cultural reality thus reinforces
> his fantasy that women's subjectivity is nonexistent or dangerous.[9]

If cultural representations of gender in which women play object to man's
subject may be connected to difficulties individuals face in learning to recognize
the separate subjectivity of others, then cultural representations of race that figure a white subject and a black other might have similar effects at the level of
interpersonal relationships. Individuals who internalize such cultural representa-

tions of race may have difficulty differentiating between their fantasy of the other and the reality of the other as a separate center of subjectivity. Indeed, the problem may be more pernicious across barriers of race and social privilege, since the two conditions I have suggested must be present for the achievement of mutual recognition may be largely absent from interactions across racial and class barriers. If members of privileged and unprivileged groups do not engage in real relationships characterized by some level of emotional resonance, subjects may simply walk away from those whose assertions of subjectivity challenge their fantasy. If members of such groups do not even come in contact with one another, there is simply no chance for the other to survive in reality attacks made on the level of fantasy.

Toni Morrison explores how such cultural representations of race do psychic damage in her novel *The Bluest Eye*. Set in rural Ohio in the 1940s, *The Bluest Eye* tells the story of Pecola Breedlove, a young African American girl who longs to have blue eyes because she believes that they will make her beautiful and win for her the love and recognition she seeks but cannot find. Morrison's characters live in a world in which whiteness is associated with beauty and power and blackness is associated with invisibility and dread. Pecola's mother Pauline internalizes these powerful representations through her "education" at the movies:

> The onliest time I be happy seem like was when I was in the picture show. Every time I got, I went. I'd go early, before the show started. They'd cut off the lights and everything be black. Then the screen would light up, and I'd move right on in them pictures. White men takin' such good care of they women, and they all dressed up in big clean houses with the bathtubs right in the same room with the toilet. Them pictures gave me a lot of pleasure, but it made coming home hard, and looking at Cholly hard.[10]

Soon after, Pauline gets a job as a maid working for the Fishers, a wealthy white family. Pauline feels a sense of power as a servant for this white family. Soon she begins to neglect her own family: "More and more she neglected her house, her children, her man—they were like the afterthoughts one has just before sleep, the early-morning and late-evening edges of her day, the edges that made the daily life with the Fishers lighter, more delicate, more lovely."[11]

Just as the black theater frames the action for the beautiful white characters on the movie screen, Pauline begins to experience her own black family as a dark, shadowy contrast to the more vitally alive and orderly world of the Fisher family. Cultural representations of race that foreground whiteness and background blackness create obstacles to acts of human recognition within Pauline's family and between the black and white characters in the novel. Morrison explores the dynamics of white misrecognition of black subjectivity as she describes what Mr. Yacobowski, a white shopkeeper, sees and does not see when little Pecola Breedlove enters his store to buy candy:

> Somewhere between retina and object, between vision and view, his eyes draw back, hesitate, and hover. At some fixed point in time and space he senses that he need not waste the effort of a glance. He does not see her because for him there is nothing to see. How can a fifty-two-year-old white immigrant storekeeper with the taste of potatoes and beer in his mouth and his mind honed on the doe-eyed Virgin Mary, his sensibilities blunted by a permanent awareness of loss, see a little black girl? Nothing in his life even suggested that the feat was possible, not to say desirable or necessary.[12]

If cultural representations of gender make it difficult to recognize the subjectivity of women, as Benjamin claims, the differences between the shopkeeper and Pecola make it still more unlikely that he will be able to recognize her as a real, external subject. Pecola's blackness evokes a fantasy of dread and aversion in the shopkeeper that absorbs him before he even looks at the little girl. Unable to distinguish between his fantasy and the real human being standing in front of him, the shopkeeper relates to the girl as if she were nothing more than a manifestation of his own dark fantasy. Morrison imagines how Pecola experiences his chilling gaze:

> She looks up and sees the vacuum where curiosity ought to lodge. . . Yet this vacuum is not new to her. It has an edge; somewhere in the bottom lid is the distaste. She has seen it lurking in the eyes of all white people. So the distaste must be for her blackness. All things in her are flux and anticipation. But her blackness is static and dread.[13]

Morrison's books offers the reader deep insights into the psychic costs of racism for everyone in American society. When one contemplates how pervasive cultural associations of whiteness with agency and power continue to be, the prospect for genuine recognition and moral dialogue across racial divides seems dim. Acknowledging the difficulty is only the first step in the struggle for human recognition. Benjamin's and Morrison's texts both suggest that we will need to work on changing cultural representations of gender and race on all levels if we want to create a social environment in which relations of mutual recognition can take root and grow.

Across race and gender groups or within them, I have suggested that care in relationships does not necessarily mean the suppression of difference in the interest of maintaining interpersonal harmony, even in the most intimate relationships. In the good-enough relationship, the expression of difference is permitted without disrupting the affective connection. The partner who stands on the receiving end of the other's self-expression neither withdraws nor retaliates, but seeks to understand the other's point of view in its own context. Through the sharing of subjective experiences, both partners develop the concrete sense that the other is truly external to oneself, and that the differences that arise between them need threaten neither their individual identities nor their relationship. While one's fantasy of the other does not disappear entirely from mental life, as one achieves recognition of the subjectivity of the other, one's fantasy may be brought into tension with the experience of the other as a separate person with feelings and projects of her own. It is in and through recognition of the difference that the other makes that we are able to enter into authentic relations of care and reciprocity. As Benjamin tells us, "The distinction between my fantasy of you and you as a real person is the very essence of connection."[14]

Can the concept of the good-enough relationship serve as a model for relationships in the democratic classroom? While there are important differences between intimate and educational settings, the two are not utterly alien to one another, and it is the similarities between them that make an adaptation of the good-enough relationship to the classroom useful. I want to suggest that in the classroom, as well as in the family, individuals have a difficult time seeing and acknowledging the separate and distinct reality of other people. We fall rather easily into responding to the other merely as a means to confirm our own sense of self. If the other does not confirm our sense of self, we experience the other as a threat and withdraw from the relationship. We have a difficult time becoming aware that in responding in this way, we are treating the other as a means to our own end, rather than an end for herself. We typically walk toward those who affirm us, and we walk away from those who seem to threaten us. The psychoanalytic lens helps us to bring our use of the other into our awareness, and the concept of the good-enough relationship suggests that we might do otherwise: We might do better in our relationships with one another.

Is it possible to suspend our desire for affirmation in our encounter with the other, to maintain the tension between this desire and our awareness of the separate subjectivity of the other, and to allow the difference that the other makes to infuse and inform our consciousness? Can we stay in dialogue across moral differences, rather than walk away from each other? It will not be easy. In fact, in many cases it may actually be painful. Parker Palmer suggests something similar when he tells us that "a learning space needs to be hospitable not to make learning painless but to make the painful things possible, things without which no learning can occur—things like exposing ignorance, testing tentative hypotheses, challenging partial or false information, and mutual criticism of thought."[15] The model of the good-enough relationship is meant to help us see that truth-seeking in the classroom through moral dialogue in the context of a caring relationship is both possible and desirable.

What would the good-enough relationship look like in an educational setting? I propose that as the model of the good-enough relationship is approximated, students come to understand themselves to be related to one another, not as soul mates, but as human beings whose dignity and uniqueness are dependent on the recognition they receive from others. Because they are caught up with one other in this way, students consider themselves to be both givers and receivers of the care that human beings need and deserve in order to thrive. We must remember that our relationships at school need not be perfect, only good enough. There will be moments when recognition will break down. We will use each other to affirm our own identities. We can become more conscious of the times when we do this, however, and we can try to do better the next time.

Second, individuals who care about one another in this way are able to share subjective states with one another. This process facilitates understanding in moral dialogue. Because we have the experience of feeling together through joint classroom activities, we take an interest in the other's point of view, and we seek to promote each other's well-being if we can. Since we take an interest in each other's subjective viewpoints, when we come together in moral dialogue, we do not instantly translate the other's argument into our own interpretive framework. Instead, we attempt to consider our partner's position within its own meaningful context. We respond to the other not simply by asking ourselves, do I agree? Should I take what she is saying as a candidate for my own thought? We also ask, what does it mean to her, given her particularity? How does she feel? Subsequently I might consider whether or not her position makes a moral claim on my thoughts, my actions, or both. Through this process of exchanging perspectives, we gain a deeper sense of how the world seems to others. Through dialogue with the other, we have the concrete experience that we are not "all there is." Our own perspective meets with its boundaries, and we begin to see that we will need to talk to each other if we wish to gain a more complete picture of the world.

Finally, there must be room within the good-enough relationship for the expression of difference. We anticipate and create space in our relationships for the expression of frustration and anger, as well as warm feelings of happiness and friendly accord. We understand that in dialogue with one another, our relationship can survive the expressions of differences that may feel to us as though they threaten our own commitments and perhaps even our identity. We know that neither partner in a conversation needs to capitulate to the position of the other in the face of disagreement in order to maintain a relationship, nor should one partner in the conversation seek to erase, deny, or ignore the claims of the other in order to protect her own position. We begin to understand that it is through caring dialogue with an other who is truly outside of our control that we come to enrich and expand our understanding of the world.

In this chapter, I have proposed an alternative to thinking about care as a form of intimacy that seeks harmony or accord with the other. Although this is a common way to think about what it means to care, it is not the only form that care might take in our private and public relationships. Consequently, once the case has been made that relationships of intimacy and accord in the classroom are likely to inhibit serious moral dialogue, we have not therefore said all that we might say about the prospects for establishing caring relationships in the classroom. As a discourse that takes seriously the significance and complexity of our affective ties with one another, psychoanalysis is a promising place to look for help in developing a more adequate concept of care and relationality. I have proposed that D.W. Winnicott's construct of the good-enough relationship can be usefully adapted to the public space where students meet and are educated to become democratic citizens. Certainly the ideal of the good-enough relationship will be difficult to realize in the classroom. In future essays, I hope to explore further some of the complexities of practice. My goal here has been to suggest the viability of a model of relationship that can help us begin to imagine how students as future citizens might engage with one another as more than just strangers, if less than soul mates.

Notes

1.   Report by Michelle Trudeau, National Public Radio, 23 May 2002.
2.   Eamonn Callan, *Creating Citizens* (New York: Oxford University Press, 1997), 207.
3.   Callan, *Creating Citizens*, 198.
4.   Callan, *Creating Citizens*, 207.
5.   D. W. Winnicott, *Playing and Reality* (1971; reprint, New York: Routledge, 1989), 12.
6.   Jessica Benjamin, *The Bonds of Love* (New York: Pantheon Books, 1988), 71.
7.   Benjamin, *The Bonds of Love*, 72.
8.   Winnicott, *Playing and Reality*, 40.
9.   Benjamin, *The Bonds of Love*, 214.
10. Toni Morrison, *The Bluest Eye* (New York: Plume, 1970), 123.
11. Morrison, *The Bluest Eye*, 127.
12. Morrison, *The Bluest Eye*, 48.
13. Morrison, *The Bluest Eye*, 49.
14. Benjamin, *The Bonds of Love*, 71.
15. Parker Palmer, *To Know as We Are Known* (San Francisco: HarperCollins, 1993), 74.

EDUCATION FOR DEMOCRACY DEMANDS "GOOD-ENOUGH" TEACHERS

Cherlyn M. Pijanowski

Magpie drew a map for Annabella and her father to show them how to reach the Kingdom of Tall Pines from their castle in the forest. "Yes, a ground map is essential," Magpie said, "though mine won't be too accurate. I know the route only as a bird flies." Magpie walked back and forth across the paper, then picked up a chalk in his beak and marked an X in the upper left-hand corner. "This X is where we are. Over here is where we want to go." He printed another X on the other side, halfway down, then raised himself a few inches off the ground and flew between the two X's. "Ah, much better. I remember it quite well now." He began to draw a line, first very straight, then curvy, and finally as wavy as the ocean . . . "This water is the Silver Sea . . . On the opposite shore is a pine forest so thick it looks like a solid wall. That is the entrance to the Kingdom of Tall Pines."[1]

Introduction

Like Magpie, I set out to create a map. Playfully, I ask, "How does one reach the "Kingdom of Relational Pedagogy" from the "castles" of traditional and progressive education? Most importantly, what guides the way within the dense relational "forest" when educational goals include human formation to make democratic relations possible? Like Magpie, I feel challenged. Not only is the road from the "castles" to the "Kingdom" long, scabrous, and, as Charles Bingham suggests, under construction. Relational Pedagogy itself is a "forest" so thick that it "looks like a solid wall." Nonetheless, as my contribution to this book I take on this cartographic work because, practically speaking, a mind map allows others to join the journey. So here I put down Xs and where necessary sketch landmarks. My process imitates Magpie's. I locate education's current position with two Xs and where pedagogy of relation wants it to go with another X.

I mark the first X at traditional education. Here, the teacher, standardized curricula, established disciplines, high-stakes testing, and systems of accountability dominate the landscape. The central goal of teacher-directed and standardized education is the formation of essential knowledge, skills, and tools that enable students to carry on Western cultural tradition.

Close by, I mark the second X at progressive education. Here, the student, problem-posing curricula, applied learning, performance-based assessment, and critical inquiry comprise the landscape. From this student-centered perspective, the purpose of education is the formation of experiences to develop learners' intellectual habits that facilitate intellectual autonomy. These habits include the ability to select and interpret knowledge, to think clearly, and to use intellectual reasoning. Far away, I mark the third X at relational education. Here, neither the teacher nor student dominates the landscape. Rather, the relational space between teacher and student, student and student, student and curricula, and student and community commands attention. Influenced by communication theory, feminist philosophy, race theory, and psychoanalytic theory, relational pedagogy proposes that education is possible only through and with human relations. In this lush terrain, therefore, the purpose of education, teaching objectives, and learning outcomes are one and the same: to form relations.

I stand back. How does one travel from traditional or progressive education to pedagogy of relation? Is it possible or even worthwhile to make the trip? As I see it, not only is it possible and worthwhile, the journey is unavoidable and morally necessary when educational aims include democracy. If this is the case, how do I map the way? In what follows, I interpret the route that a veteran teacher and her students take to the "Kingdom of Relation." I don't offer a full exploration of their excursion in this chapter, so like Magpie's map, mine "won't be too accurate." My intention is only to provide general direction to relational pedagogy and a broad sense of what education for democratic relation demands of teachers.

Magpie to the Rescue

In her book *You Can't Say You Can't Play*, Vivian Paley, a veteran primary school teacher and author of books about her experiences in the classroom, huddles her kindergartners around a rug to discuss a recurring problem. The children listen with wide eyes as their teacher tells them, "Something unhappy took place today in the blocks." Paley continues, "Clara was made to feel unwanted. Not wanted." The teacher gets everyone's attention when she admits that she "couldn't decide what to do about Clara's unhappiness."[2] The children look over to Clara to see if she is still unhappy. Paley then tells the children that she is thinking about implementing a new classroom rule, "You can't say you can't play," designed to protect children from the practice of exclusion and to "create a space where you are always asked, 'Do you want to play?'"[3] Her announcement is met by disbelief.

Before Paley implements the rule, she hears the arguments the children offer against the rule. She eventually elevates the problem of exclusion—

expressed in "you can't play"—for critical review first by her students, then by children in the higher grades. She explains to her disbelieving five-year-olds, "We're talking about it, getting opinions, thinking about it, wondering how it will work."[4] Lisa is the child in Paley's classroom who protests the loudest against the rule. Lisa's argument contains first a narrative of possession, then one of fear and jealousy. The logic of her argument initially goes something like this: If I design the game, the game is mine, and as owner of the play I should be able to decide who gets to be included. If I am required to include others, then I am not the person in charge of my play, which makes me sad, and I cannot play if I am sad. If you can't be the boss, "then what's the whole point of playing?" Lisa asks.[5] Clearly, Lisa wants to be able to "push Clara out one day and Smita the next and Cynthia after that." Paley's proposed rule challenges Lisa's perception of play as a space where children "empower bosses and reject classmates." Paley settles the children to hear the latest chapter in a story she spins about a bird named Magpie. The Magpie story, a welcomed interruption to the classroom deliberation over the rule of "You can't say you can't play," transports Paley's kindergartners (and her readers) into the make-believe world of Tall Pines, where Magpie rescues those who are lonely or frightened and tells them stories "to raise their spirits." Today, a new character emerges. It is Beatrix, whom Magpie describes as an improper witch because she is "not mean enough." As Magpie puts it, "She can be naughty . . . especially when she's jealous, but mostly she wants to play just as you do."[6] We pick up the story when Magpie and his new friends, Annabella and her father, Prince Kareem, reach the Kingdom of Tall Pines where Beatrix lives. Annabella anxiously waits to meet Beatrix, the "not mean enough" witch who saved her feathered friend's life, but Beatrix does not appear. "Beatrix is never ready to greet anyone new in her dear Magpie's life," exclaims Alexandra, who lives in Tall Pines. "When [Beatrix] first met me, she tried to turn me into a frog, but luckily that was too hard for her." Everyone laughed, not knowing that the "very jealous Beatrix, glowering at the newcomers," is "hidden nearby behind a tree" listening all along. Beatrix whispered to herself, "Don't be too sure of me, Magpie. I'm not as nice as you think I am."[7]

Paley closes her notebook. The children know the story will continue tomorrow. They leave the rug, but the fictional character, Magpie, stays on their minds as they sort out the classroom controversy surrounding the rule "You can't say you can't play." Lisa, for example, joins Paley at the story table, where children dictate to Paley stories of their own creation. At the table, Lisa dictates this story: "One day a kitty that had no mother or father and was an orphan asked if she could be a sister and they said yes. The end." Paley points out to Lisa that in the stories Lisa authors she lets everyone play. Lisa responds to Paley's observation with one of her own. "Beatrix is jealous, you know," as if she and Paley had "been discussing Magpie's witch friend all along." She adds, "That's the reason she thinks she's not nice. Jealous people don't feel nice."

As Lisa talks she draws pictures. As she draws, Paley reminds her that "Beatrix does do nice things." Paley invites Lisa to draw illustrations for the Magpie story. Lisa sits patiently drawing several pictures of Beatrix, trying to get her illustration just right. Paley watches Lisa, then recalls that earlier in the day Lisa had made a kind gesture toward another child. Paley compliments Lisa on her good deed. In reply, Lisa asks Paley, "Who is nicer, me or Beatrix?" She immediately follows this question with another, "Is she going to hurt Annabella?" Before Paley formulates a response, Lisa jumps up and enthusiastically remarks, "Oh, no! Magpie won't ever let her be mean to Annabella. I just know that," then runs off to play.[8] Eventually, Paley's most vocal resister, Lisa, begins inviting children into her play rather than rejecting them.[9]

Education with and for Democratic Character Normation

To a cartographer wanting to understand the nature of pedagogy that leads children into democratic relations, what direction does Paley's example provide? How does Paley lead Lisa from relations based on domination to relations based on mutual regard? To begin, I consider the possibility that Paley does this by taking a pathway that runs between the castles of traditional and progressive education. Perhaps she leads Lisa into relations based on mutual regard by teaching traditional content through progressively experiential methods, perhaps resulting in the development of democratic character. I make several observations, which create the illusion that relational pedagogy lies somewhere between traditional and progressive education and is therefore accessible from either spot.

Paley's instruction communicates traditional concepts and values of American liberal democracy, such as inclusion, fairness, and deliberation. Content also addresses essential democratic truths, such as that all children have an equal right to learn, play freely, and be happy in school so long as such pursuits don't obstruct others who pursue the same rights. Paley teaches this traditional content through progressive and experiential methods. She takes a problem-posing approach to learning that builds on progressively organized experiences, cultivates critical thinking, and teaches children how to democratically resolve disagreements. The rule, "You can't say you can't play," builds from and critically examines classroom themes of meanness and play. Paley's transition from a discussion about friendship into story about a friendly bird that rescues those who are lonely and sad further extends her children's experiences. Then during individualized instruction with Lisa, Paley strengthens the connections between the idea of the rule, the practice of exclusion, and the experience of play. Learning in Paley's classroom is active and focused simultaneously on the present and on the future. Instruction is meaningful and relevant to the students' experiences. With Paley, as with progressive education, the child is the starting point for the curriculum. Paley works from her students' experiences of control and rejection to develop rich curriculum consisting of the rule, story, and classroom discussion teaching the subject matter of friendship and inclusion.

Since Paley develops "You can't say you can't play" and the Magpie story to create a democratic classroom normation that enables children to "depend on the kindness of strangers," I'm tempted to say that Paley's instructional approach teaches more than knowledge and problem solving essential to democratic social life.[10] Her approach also develops the deliberative and moral conscience of her children. I consider, for example, how Paley's instruction provides a practical translation of Amy Gutman's theory of democratic education.[11] Gutman proposes that the "primary democratic aim of primary education" is "the development of deliberative character"[12] through "exemplary" and "didactic" instruction."[13] In Gutman's view, deliberative character forms through a combination of moral content and developed capacity for reasoning. As she sees it, both are "necessary, neither sufficient, for creating democratic citizens." Though "inculcating character and teaching moral reasoning by no means exhaust the purposes of primary education in a democracy," Gutman argues that "together they constitute its core political purpose."[14]

Consistent with Gutman's conception of democratic education, Paley teaches children the cognitive process skills of democratic deliberation, which are critical to democratic relations. The discussion she facilitates defines and redefines the problem of how to "create a space where you are always asked, 'Do you want to play?' and where you can depend on the kindness of strangers."[15] The deliberated rule, "You can't say you can't play," involves questions of right action: "Is the new rule fair?" "Can it work?"[16] And, "What if someone doesn't have a few good friends? Wouldn't my rule give them some protection?"[17] Paley guarantees each child a fair hearing and she models how to seek to understand the positions of others. She leaves no one in the classroom community out as she exposes the proposed rule to public scrutiny. Everyone responsible for enacting the decision is at the rug for discussion. Likewise, Paley approaches the larger school community to learn from older children their thoughts on whether her class should implement the rule. She then shares these responses with her kindergartners, demonstrating deliberative thoroughness. Moreover, following Gutman, it seems that Paley inculcates character and teaches moral reasoning through "exemplary" and "didactic" instruction. It can be said that Paley, as an exemplary teacher who is loved and respected, shapes the character and skills of children both by demonstration and by the rules that regulate the associations of the class to which her children belong. As a didactic teacher, Paley enables

her children to acquire the knowledge and tools to participate in Western cultural tradition. She uses the rule and deliberation to develop her students' "capacities for criticism, rational argument, and decision-making." She teaches her
children "how to think logically, to argue coherently and fairly, and to consider
the relevant alternatives before coming to conclusions." [18] Paley explains that
the new rule "gives us a useful perspective from which to view our actions." It
"examines a specific form of meanness and uses the imagery of play to do so."[19]
I notice that every time Paley and her children "analyze the logic of the rule"
they also "think about the logic of their behavior."[20]

While I could regard Paley's classroom narrative as a performance of democratic political education consistent with Gutman's definition, I might also
think about it as a case of moral education. I consider, for example, Paley's instruction in light of Thomas F. Green's theory of moral education. In *Voices:
The Educational Formation of Conscience,* Green claims that "moral education has to
do with an acquired temper of the self" and the formation of conscience
through the acquisition of norms that effectively govern behavior.[21] He defines
norms as rules of conduct that prescribe how to act in particular settings rather
than "the formulation of a modal pattern of behavior."[22] He argues that norms
"come to possess us" through human action and activities, and participation in
social institutions.[23] Normation, he claims, is "the central business of moral
education."[24] Unlike notions of compliance, obedience, and observance,
Green's conception of normation connects to an "attitude of caring . . . the attitude that rectitude matters."[25] In other words, one must care whether or not
and how one's conduct is in accordance with social norms. According to Green,
normation requires the development of a multivoiced conscience. Conscience is
"reflexive judgment about things that matter" and "speaks" to us in multiple
voices: the conscience of craft, the conscience of membership, the voice of
memory, and the conscience of imagination.[26]

Mapping Green's conception of moral education onto Paley's classroom
narrative suggests that Paley's traditional and progressive approaches take her
and her children into the neighborhood of moral education as Green delineates
it. Paley's instruction seems to develop among her children a multivoiced conscience. She gives her students time to sort through the issues involved in the
practice of rejection and in the enforcement of the new rule. Paley doesn't con-
demn Lisa for her bossy behavior, but instead provides time and opportunities
for Lisa to question and reconsider it. Paley doesn't want her children to merely
observe "You can't say you can't play" out of compliance or obedience; rather,
she wants the rule to become a habit. Toward this end, she seems to cultivate
the voices of conscience necessary to norm acquisition. When she allows her
children to coauthor a chapter in the Magpie story (the children import the rule
"You can't say you can't play" into the "'Kingdom of Tall Pines"'), she culti-

vates the voice of craft. When she brings Clara's private unhappiness into the public arena for discussion, she cultivates the voice of membership. When she introduces the new rule telling children what they cannot do, she cultivates the voice of sacrifice. When she introduces the Magpie story to help her children to think self-reflectively about the classroom controversy, she cultivates the voice of memory. When she imports the rule into the "Kingdom of Tall Pines," she cultivates the voice of imagination, helping her children to visualize what the new rule means and how it can work.

While Green's conception of moral education and Gutman's theory of democratic education bring into relief ways in which Paley's instruction might form deliberative character and impress upon students "voices of conscience," I become disillusioned when this pedagogical thought-path turns into a thicket of political character normation rather than the "Kingdom of Relation." Surely, sharing core beliefs, common knowledge, values, voices of conscience, habits of mind, and deliberative abilities creates a clearing for relations based on mutual regard. However, deliberative character normation does not necessarily lead those who have been so normed into democratic relations. People can, and many do, resist entering relations, particularly with others who are not like they are. Paley observes, for example, that Lisa prefers to play with blonde girls and excludes those who are "in some way different from the children she has known."[27] Lisa admits, "There's some people I don't like."[28] Moreover, when relations with despised, feared, different others become inescapable, people can, and many do, use those relationships in exploitative, manipulative, objectifying, and self-serving ways that may even appear democratic. For example, shortly after Paley implements the rule "You can't say you can't play," Lisa crusades for the old order. She suggests "in her most polite voice" that the class make a slight but significant modification to the rule, or as she puts it, "not too much change it, but kind of change." Rationally and diplomatically, she offers a compromise: "We could say yes you could play if you really really really want to play so much that you just take the part the person in charge wants you to be."[29] In other words, Lisa wants to manipulate the rule in order to be able to "legally" transform those whom she does not like into play characters that extend from her as "owner" of play.

Reaching the entrance of the relational "forest" from the regions of traditional and progressive education, therefore, demands "working through" the political thicket of character normation. Such work is difficult and uncomfortable, as Cris Mayo argues in this book. It is difficult because it means coming to terms with the fact that wishes for freedom and progress coexist with racial, gender, and sexual hierarchy and exclusion, which reflect racist, sexist, and homophobic fears and desires that are "other" to democracy. It is unpleasant because it means learning what may be unbearable to know about our selves. Toni

Morrison's *Playing in the Dark* facilitates such critical work.[30] Although Morrison operates as a literary rather than an educational theorist, her brilliant essay provides a transitional space where it becomes possible to poke through political character normation in order to bring the "Kingdom of Relation" into view.

In *Playing in the Dark*, Morrison investigates racism and the construction of whiteness in the literary imagination. She works in the shadows of traditional American literature, where she endeavors to understand ways in which "a non-white, African-like presence or persona was constructed in the United States, and the imaginative uses this fabricated presence served."[31] Her investigation leads her into the canon of American literature, where she finds a variety of examples to illustrate how white American writers have objectified black American characters in order to establish differentness or otherness, and to partially construct the meaning of whiteness and the American self through such otherness. She points out how the white literary imagination has rendered black characters as enslaved, repulsive, helpless, voiceless, history-less, damned, and a mistake in evolution, in order to identify whites as the exact opposite: free, desirable, licensed and powerful, vocal, historical, innocent, and a progressive fulfillment of destiny.[32] Morrison's purpose for writing the essay is twofold. She wants to make accessible the complex methods in which white authors have used blackness to explore white fears and desires and shore up an admirable self-image. More importantly, she wants to illuminate ways in which "[a] genderized, sexualized, wholly racialized world" restricts and enables literary imagination.[33]

Importing Morrison's analysis of literary imagination onto Paley's narrative offers rich opportunity to comprehend the inadequacy of political character normation that traditional and progressive approaches achieve while opening new ground from which to appreciate the relational force of Paley's pedagogy. Morrison's work calls attention to the reality that public education takes place in an imperfect and undemocratic world in which "agendas for personal freedom" combine with "devastating racial oppression" to "present a singular landscape" for students like Lisa.[34] Morrison's analysis opens space to consider how this social, political, and economic landscape might affect the mind, imagination, and behavior of learners as well as teachers. Morrison's investigation summons forth the possibility that Lisa needs those whom she excludes to embody her own fear of rejection, just as white American writers have used black enslaved characters to contain white fear of freedom. Although democratic content, moral education, and progressively organized experiences are important, Morrison's project illuminates why content, experiences, and political character normation alone do not make democratic relations possible. In addition, democratic relations require certain psychological and imaginative capacities. These capacities include mutual recognition instead of objectification, the ability to articulate needs and feelings instead of unconscious projection of fears and desires, respect of others instead of contempt of others, and trust of strangers instead of fear of different others. These capacities, however, cannot grow strong, if at all, on the singular landscape that Morrison describes. In order to develop, they require a range of reciprocal relations rich enough to undermine the influences of a "genderized, sexualized, wholly racialized world."

With the light that Morrison's work casts, I return to Paley's narrative. How does Paley's practice skirt the thicket of political character normation? How does she develop the psychological and imaginative capacities that democracy requires? These questions provoke a radically different reading. Perhaps Paley initiates the turn away from political character normation when she tracks emotion, desire, and object relations on the pathway of human formation. Perhaps she leads Lisa into relations based on mutual regard through instruction that weaves between self and other, between the classroom and the Magpie story, between the stories children tell and the stories they act out. And perhaps such instruction helps Lisa to create a shared reality that she uses as a means to invite others into her play without domination. Since theorists of education and democracy seldom take this approach, I advance slowly. I make some initial observations, then return to fill in with theoretical detail.

Education with and for Human Formation

Exploring Paley's narrative from the pathway of human formation expands the landscape of education. New sights come into view. I notice, for example, that Paley pays close attention to how her students feel. How children feel matters because, as Paley explains, "children who are told they can't play don't learn well. They might become too sad to pay attention." [35] Paley, therefore, teaches her children the importance of feelings—that how they and others feel is important. She also teaches them how to give voice to feelings. Paley does this when she responds to Clara's tears by gathering all the children together to discuss the unhappy occurrence in the block area where Clara was made to feel unwanted when she was told "you can't play." And, when she later tells Lisa, "I agree with Angelo. He said when you're not allowed to play you feel lonely and you get water in your eyes. And if you're lonely and sad I'm afraid you can't learn very much or behave very well." [36] Along with responding to the problem of rejection in terms of Clara's feelings, Paley discusses the problem of rejection in terms of the emotions the problem rouses in her as the teacher. Paley, for instance, shares with her students her own frustration that she doesn't know exactly what to do about Clara's unhappiness. [37]

Another feature of Paley's instruction stands out: She not only attends to and gives voice to feelings, but she also uses the content of her own emotions as an instructional resource. Consider, for example, how her personal experience shapes her instructional response to the conflict in the block corner. Paley admits to readers in her reflections about the conflict that her personal experiences with rejection make her particularly sensitive to Clara's sadness. She explains that from kindergarten on, she did not feel at ease in school, though she did well. "I can still recall the clouded faces of outcast children in the classrooms of my childhood, and also the faces of the confident ones who seemed to know exactly how everything must be done."[38] She then confesses, "To be accurate, I didn't really attend kindergarten." She started but then was removed from kindergarten because her teacher thought she wasn't ready. The teacher told Paley's mother, "Your daughter just sits outside the circle and watches." Paley recounts, "Much later, when I asked my mother why she didn't insist that I remain and learn how to enter the magic circle, she shrugged" and said, "But that was the teacher telling me." Paley offers a different explanation: that she sat outside the circle because she didn't know how to enter the group.[39] In effect, she helps us to see that it isn't only Clara's unhappiness that provokes Paley to tell the Magpie story and create the rule, "You can't say you can't play." Additionally, a personal wish to resolve an old conflict shapes her instructional response.

Along with acknowledging and responding to feelings, I observe that Paley follows feelings to their relational center. By this I mean she pays attention to how her students (and indeed she herself) associate and attach to the world and the environmental conditions that elicit those associations and attachments. Consider, for example, Paley's interactions with Lisa around the story table. Paley notices that although Lisa protests the loudest against the rule, she always dictates to Paley fictional stories in which everyone plays. This observation causes Paley to wonder about Lisa's association with the rule. She becomes curious about the feelings and relations that motivate Lisa's determination to keep certain children out of her actual play. Similarly, Paley wonders about Lisa's association with Beatrix, the "not mean enough" witch. After Lisa verbalizes her concern to Paley about Beatrix's meanness and draws several pictures of the fictional character, trying to get her rendering just right, Paley asks herself, "Would [Lisa, like Beatrix] tell Annabella she can't play, preferring Alexandra?" She then marvels at Lisa's attachment to Magpie. She notices that "[Lisa] likes Magpie and trusts him. His is the first picture she draws for the book." This triggers Paley to ask herself, "Who is this Magpie who won't let Beatrix be mean?" She imagines that for Lisa he is someone "apparently more powerful than jealousy and more dependable than impulse and caprice." She guesses that Lisa wants her to be "more like Magpie and not allow her to be mean even when she is jealous of playmates or uncomfortable with strangers." Paley therefore subjects the rule to a relational test: "When Lisa accepts Angelo into her play or story, it will be a sign that the rule is working."[40]

Although from the perspectives of traditional and progressive education these observations may seem tangential to education, theories of human formation provide conceptual details that indicate otherwise. Human formation theory is interested in how feelings, the development of human subjectivity, and object attachment are interrelated. Human formation cannot take place outside the context of relational attachments that grow the capacity for mutual recognition, the ability to articulate needs and feelings, respect for others, and trust. Theories of human formation explain the psychological structure of these capacities, how they develop, what interferes with their development, and how we use them to live fully and responsively, recording and taking pleasure in our experiences of self and others without domination of or complete acquiescence to an other.

Feminist theorist Nancy Chodorow provides a particularly useful theory in *The Power of Feelings*.[41] Her theory proposes that when Paley tracks feelings and object attachment, she tracks relations. Moreover, it suggests that when Paley responds to and works from emotion and desire, and attends to object attachment, she practices pedagogy of relation to make learning and human formation possible. Chodorow explains that feelings emerge in self-other fields in which object relations are always at the center. She defines feelings as feeling-based stories and fantasies "that constitute our unconscious inner life and motivate our attempts to change that inner life to reduce anxiety and other uncomfortable or frightening affects or to put such uncomfortable affects outside the self."[42] Feelings, she explains, move by way of transference, projection, and introjection, psychic capacities that "develop and unfold virtually from birth, in a context of interaction with others."[43] Chodorow explains that without feelings and the opportunity to express them, it is not possible to interpret external experiences and create personal meaning. Without feelings, learning is not possible.[44] Since feelings fuel "everyday, life-constructing meaning," and "shape interpersonal relationships, personal projects, work, and the constructions of cultural meanings and practices," she argues that they must never be reduced to simple components but must be investigated in "their richest complexity."[45]

While such investigation is crucial to human formation, human formation theory suggests that it is also crucial to democracy. The practice of engaging and examining beliefs, desires, hopes, and fears brings them to the surface of conscious awareness. Here they can be accounted for, reconsidered, and more productively directed instead of expressed in disruptive, violent, and unfathomable ways. However, in order for such investigations to bear democratic fruit within the relational "forest," they must be of a good-enough nature and conducted by practitioners of relational pedagogy who are no more and no less than good-

enough. According to D. W. Winnicott, "good-enough" means creating conditions that nurture the capacity to use others to become a self, but not in an exploitative way. [46] After providing a synopsis of Winnicott's theory, I return to
Paley's narrative in order to look for evidence of teaching practice that is good-
enough.

In *Playing and Reality,* Winnicott elaborates a relational theory of human
formation. Winnicott's theory, like that of Chodorow, accounts for the dynamic
relationship between internal and external experience. He explains that the constant human challenge is keeping inner and outer reality separate yet interrelated. He theorizes that this task requires the presence of three elements. First,
an "intermediate area of experience," which he locates between the individual
and his or her environment.[47] This area of experiencing, "to which inner reality
and external life both contribute," is "not challenged, because no claim is made
on its behalf except that it shall exist as a resting-place."[48] It is here that a person makes the transition from relating to an object as a me-extension, to recognizing an object as an external phenomenon and as an entity in its own right.
Winnicott uses the concepts of transitional objects and transitional phenomenon to designate this third space.[49] He gives us the experience of play as an example of a transitional site where "the interplay of personal psychic reality and
the experience of control of actual objects" take place.[50] He explains that play is
fundamental to human flourishing. The experience of play provides opportunities for creativity, enrichment, and removal of blocks to development.[51]
Through playing, children develop, change, and rearrange what things mean to
them.

Winnicott claims that interweaving inner and outer reality also requires the
capacity for illusion, which enables us to "create, think up, devise, originate, and
produce" transitional space and objects.[52] As Winnicott puts it, without illusion
"there is no meaning for the human being in the idea of a relationship with an
object that is perceived by others as external to that being."[53] Winnicott points
out, however, that illusion is not possible without a third element: a "good-
enough mother" (or good-enough parent). Winnicott theorizes that the good-
enough mother works in opposing directions toward the infant. Initially, she
completely adapts to the infant's needs, contributing to the deception that she is
an extension of the child. Gradually, the good-enough mother pulls away,
adapting less and less completely as the child's ability to tolerate failure of adaptation increases. In effect, the good-enough mother contributes to both disillusionment and an infant's "growing ability to recognize and accept
[interdependent] reality."[54] A too-good mother or a not-good-enough one, on
the other hand, both obstruct self-formation and interfere with the development of an autonomous self. The former does so by contributing to the illusion

that the world is an extension of "me" while the later provides so much disillusionment that the child never learns to trust the outside world.[55]

These three elements, Winnicott theorizes, combine to create a good-enough environment, which is necessary to help a child to transition from object relating to object usage. In object relating, the subject finds him/herself in the object through projection and identification. In object usage, the same is true but with the new feature that the subject regards the object not as a projective entity but as an external phenomenon and a thing in its own right.[56] According to Winnicott, "a capacity to use an object is more sophisticated than a capacity to relate to objects," because object usage "implies that the object is part of external reality."[57] He theorizes that the steps of autonomous development are: subject relates to object; as object becomes external, subject uses and destroys object; object survives destruction by the subject; and thereafter the subject recognizes object as an entity in its own right and outside the subject's omnipotent control.[58] A good-enough environment, explains Winnicott, facilitates this development when it accurately returns to the child what is there or what has happened.[59] He refers to this process as mirroring and theorizes that mirroring is essential to human formation and makes possible the transition from object relating to object usage. Mirroring allows children to see themselves, and a child must be able to see him or herself in the parent's [teacher's] face before he or she can develop the ability to relate to others as not-me. When a face reflects what is there to be seen, a child can then feel real. Winnicott points out that "feeling real . . . is finding a way to exist as oneself, and to relate to objects as oneself, and to have a self into which to retreat for relaxation."[60]

Following Winnicott, it seems fitting to consider Paley as a "good-enough teacher" insofar as her practice meets the three conditions that Winnicott delineates. First, Paley protects and establishes intermediate areas of experience for the children in her classroom. When she creates the rule "You can't say you can't play," she ensures that children have open access to the "potential space" of play.[61] However, she does not suddenly impose the rule, nor does she introduce it alone. This is because her children (and indeed Paley herself) cannot imagine how the new rule will work. She therefore creates and introduces Magpie and the Tale of Tall Pines as transitional objects to engage her students' capacity (and her own) to imagine both why the classroom rule is necessary and how it can work. Second, Paley builds her students' capacity for illusion and disillusion. As she spins the Tale of Tall Pines she establishes potential space between the rule and the Tale of Tall Pines. Here children rest as they travel on the wings of Magpie from illusion to disillusion, from subjective dependence—captured in the statement "You can't play"—toward intersubjective independence, woven in the principle "You can't say you can't play." Third, as a good-enough teacher, Paley does not completely adapt to Lisa's bossy behavior, as a too-good teacher might by allowing it to continue without question. Yet at the same time, as a not-good-enough teacher might, she does not abandon Lisa or render her invisible or voiceless by ignoring her strong feelings to implement the rule for her "own good." Rather, as a good-enough teacher she listens to Lisa, recognizes her feelings, and provides the conditions that enable Lisa to externalize the feelings and relations that motivate bossiness in order to destroy it. What makes this possible for Lisa is Paley's "good-enough environmental provision."[62]

As a good-enough teacher, Paley provides a good-enough environment that enables Lisa to move from projective identification toward a "world of shared reality" that she can use and that can "feed back other-than-me substance."[63] Paley achieves this in three ways through story, "children's preferred frame of reference."[64] She writes down the stories that children tell her, but writing the stories is not enough. She also has the children act out their stories in an activity that she calls "play story acting." Acting out the stories, she says, gives children "a direct connection" to each other. In this activity, authors give other children the opportunity to play and "to take the role they wish."[65] As other children weave their ideas and imaginations, the subjective story becomes intersubjective, reflecting "other-than-me substance" to both the story author and story actors. Finally, Paley tells a story of her own creation. As she turns the Tale of Tall Pines, she invents Magpie and a range of characters—some more vulnerable than others, and puts the characters and their voices "out there" for her kindergartners to consider as possible reflections of themselves. Although Paley provides the mirrors of Magpie characters, the children as listeners do the interpretive work. Lisa's interactions with Paley at the story table provide a useful illustration. Recall that at the story table Lisa draws pictures of Beatrix, the "not mean enough" witch. Paley wonders what meaning Lisa develops from this interesting character, but Paley does not need to ask. Lisa compares herself to Beatrix with the question, "Who is nicer? Me or Beatrix?" Paley responds that both Lisa and Beatrix can be mean but both do nice things too. Beatrix, in fact, once saved Magpie's life. Lisa then states emphatically that jealous people don't feel nice. This question and comment suggest that Lisa's initial argument of possession against the rule "You can't say you can't play" has more to it. Beneath her meanness lay jealous feelings, fear of exclusion, and desire to not hurt or mistreat other children. With the help of Beatrix, Lisa discovers this part of herself previously unknown, and develops the ability to identify and express emotions at "the soul of a controversy."[66] And with the help of Magpie, she develops the capacity to tolerate the frustration of disillusion along with the ability to accept Hiroka, Jennifer, and Angelo, previously excluded children, into her play.[67] In other words, with the support of a good-enough classroom environment, which provides objects that Lisa can use to see herself, feel real, and relate to others as "not-me," Lisa develops the capacity to enter relations based on mutual regard.

Mapping Winnicott's notions of the good-enough mother and good-enough environmental provision onto Paley's classroom narrative takes me far from the "castles" of traditional and progressive education and deep into the "Kingdom of Relation." Here, I move between the outer object world of the classroom and the inner subject world of learners and teachers, between curriculum and instruction and emotions and desires, becoming keenly aware of relation's fundamental role in human formation. However, with Winnicott's guidance, I'm able to see both the relational forest and the varied and tangled trees of relation. The concepts such as good-enough, too-good, and not-good-enough help me to understand that relation is not necessarily good. Indeed, exclusion in education is as relational as inclusion. For this reason pedagogy of relation must consider democracy and human formation that makes democratic relations possible as educational aims. When pedagogy of relation does this, it places huge demands on those who teach. When educational goals include democracy and democratic character formation, pedagogy of relation requires teachers and environments that are "good-enough."

Paley's classroom narrative provides a concrete example of "good-enough." With Winnicott, I deepen my appreciation for the democratic journey on which Paley and her children embark, and develop a greater understanding of the knowledge, skills, and capabilities such a journey requires. I come to see that Paley doesn't educate for democratic relations only through curriculum that teaches traditional democratic values. Rather, she educates for democracy when she enacts a rule that gives everyone equal access to an activity fundamental to human flourishing—play. Likewise, I come to see that it is not the process through which the rule gets enacted that is democratic. Rather, it is the content of the rule—the object of play and the relation between it and subjectivity or human formation—that matters.

By proposing and enacting the rule, Paley as a good-enough teacher provides for the cultivation and expression of student voice in a radically democratic sense. As a good-enough teacher, Paley cultivates student voice through a good-enough environmental provision that gives back to a child what is there, which makes self-formation possible. Without a self, a child is voiceless, and without a voice, democratic representation and deliberation are not possible. Paley not only gives Lisa a voice, she also makes it possible for the sad and excluded children to speak when they, like Lisa, find Magpie characters with which to identify.

Finally, with Winnicott's guidance, it becomes clear that it is not experiential pedagogy that enables Lisa to create and enter relations of mutual regard.

Nor is it deliberation or moral character normation. Rather, it is the "good-enough" teacher whose relation to Lisa mirrors to Lisa her self-content that enables Lisa to throw herself into democratic relations. In other words, it is education that promotes self-formation and that makes it possible for Lisa to reach out from within, to throw herself into relations that are based on a mutual experience of inclusion. Only "good-enough" teaching—education with and for relation—is capable of this. Anything less and anything more than "good-enough" teaching wouldn't be deserving of the name education. Rather, anything less and anything more would foster miseducation and/or indoctrination to produce compliance. It would promote the formation of undemocratic characters that favor domination or subjugation over democracy. Finally, anything less and anything more would obstruct self-formation, endangering human dignity—the heart of democracy—and block the possibility of democratic relations.

Notes

1. Vivian Gussin Paley, *You Can't Say You Can't Play* (Cambridge: Harvard University Press, 1992), 29.
2. Paley, *You Can't Say You Can't Play*, 13.
3. Paley, *You Can't Say You Can't Play*, 57.
4. Paley, *You Can't Say You Can't Play*, 56.
5. Paley, *You Can't Say You Can't Play*, 20.
6. Paley, *You Can't Say You Can't Play*, 23–24.
7. Paley, *You Can't Say You Can't Play*, 64.
8. Paley, *You Can't Say You Can't Play*, 65.
9. Paley, *You Can't Say You Can't Play*, 4.
10. Paley, *You Can't Say You Can't Play*, 57.
11. Amy Gutman, *Democratic Education* (Princeton, NJ: Princeton University Press, 1999).
12. Gutman, *Democratic Education*, 52.
13. Gutman, *Democratic Education*, 50.
14. Gutman, *Democratic Education*, 51–53.
15. Paley, *Democratic Education*, 57.
16. Paley, *Democratic Education*, 33.
17. Paley, *Democratic Education*, 60.
18. Gutman, *Democratic Education*, 50.
19. Paley, *You Can't Say You Can't Play*, 114.
20. Paley, *You Can't Say You Can't Play*, 115.
21. Thomas F. Green, *Voices: The Educational Formation of Conscience* (Notre Dame, IN: Notre Dame University Press, 1999), 3.
22. Green, *Voices*, 33.
23. Green, *Voices*, 48–49.

24. Green, *Voices*, 26.
25. Green, *Voices*, 40.
26. Green, *Voices*, 61, 90.
27. Paley, *You Can't Say You Can't Play*, 68.
28. Paley, *You Can't Say You Can't Play*, 82.
29. Paley, *You Can't Say You Can't Play*, 94.
30. Toni Morrison, *Playing in the Dark: Whiteness and the Literary Imagination* (New York: Vintage Books, 1992).
31. Morrison, *Playing in the Dark*, 6.
32. Morrison, *Playing in the Dark*, 52.
33. Morrison, *Playing in the Dark*, 4.
34. Morrison, *Playing in the Dark*, xiii.
35. Paley, *You Can't Say You Can't Play*, 28.
36. Paley, *You Can't Say You Can't Play*, 83.
37. Paley, *You Can't Say You Can't Play*, 13.
38. Paley, *You Can't Say You Can't Play*, 10.
39. Paley, *You Can't Say You Can't Play*, 11.
40. Paley, *You Can't Say You Can't Play*, 82.
41. Nancy Chodorow, *The Power of Feelings: Personal Meaning in Psychoanalysis, Gender, and Culture* (New Haven & London: Yale University Press, 1999).
42. Chodorow, *The Power of Feelings*, 13.
43. Chodorow, *The Power of Feelings*, 14.
44. Chodorow, *The Power of Feelings*, 17.
45. Chodorow, *The Power of Feelings*, 240.
46. D.W. Winnicott, *Playing and Reality* (New York: Routledge, 1971), 94.
47. Winnicott, *Playing and Reality*, 2.
48. Winnicott, *Playing and Reality*, 89.
49. Winnicott, *Playing and Reality*, 2.
50. Winnicott, *Playing and Reality*, 47.
51. Winnicott, *Playing and Reality*, 50.
52. Winnicott, *Playing and Reality*, 2.
53. Winnicott, *Playing and Reality*, 11.
54. Winnicott, Playing and Reality, 3.
55. Winnicott, *Playing and Reality*, 89.
56. Winnicott, *Playing and Reality*, 89.
57. Winnicott, *Playing and Reality*, 94.
58. Winnicott, *Playing and Reality*, 90.
59. Winnicott, *Playing and Reality*, 61.
60. Winnicott, *Playing and Reality*, 117.
61. Winnicott, *Playing and Reality*, 100.
62. Winnicott, *Playing and Reality*, 71.
63. Winnicott, *Playing and Reality*, 94.
64. Paley, *You Can't Say You Can't Play*, 4.
65. Paley, *You Can't Say You Can't Play*, 84.
66. Paley, *You Can't Say You Can't Play*, 4.
67. Paley, *You Can't Say You Can't Play*, 117, 128.

RELATIONS ARE DIFFICULT

Cris Mayo

There has been much attention recently to the resistance on the part of white or other majority students to anti-bias curriculum. Characterized as "nonengagement" by Chavez Chavez and O'Donnell, the difficulties of bringing majority students into a fuller understanding of their privilege and their active ignorance of social divisions is a key obstacle to pulling white students out of their comfort with the world as they see it into the activity of challenging social inequities.[1] At the base of these concerns over dominant students' resistance is a realization that those students are not relating to the topic of bias. Perhaps because of their social status, some dominant students are disinterested in finding out how their passive acceptance of privilege means that their relationships with nondominant people will be difficult and always negotiated through the experience of power imbalance. In order to address the problem of dominant students opting out of forging relationships across the divides of race, gender, class, and sexuality, some multicultural and anti-bias educators have attempted to make the classroom a place apart from the world of social fractures, a place where dialogue across difference can happen outside the context of difficult relations. I will argue that the attempts to make relationships less difficult does a disservice to the abilities of students to thrash out the challenges that they face in a world rife with inequalities.

While the kind of approach to diversity that reassures students that "we're all different from one another" is one way to engage students, it does so by first providing comfort in everyone's equal participation in the issue of diversity. The comforting form of multiculturalism paints the world as diverse, knowable, and potentially pacific in its unproblematic leveling of different subjectivities. This sort of diversity education seeks to address injustice by making all students feel at home in a world of diversity. It is my contention that the figure of "home" and "domestic relations" does much to derail what I take be necessary components of antiracist education. In short, these homeward trends in education forestall precisely the sort of alienation toward ourselves and others that would better facilitate an examination of the power relations undergirding racialized subjectivity and race relations. In addition, by positing some sort of home as the goal and space of education, students are discouraged from entering into relations with others out in the world. So I want to argue that education ought not be home. By doing so, I am not suggesting students learn alone, but that they learn together with others with whom they may not find domestic bliss.

In this chapter I trace out the relationship among the themes of aporia, the uncanny, and vertigo, and use these connections to criticize a trend that links knowledge with the desire for home. First, I examine the necessary break with habit that marks the beginning of thinking and acting differently, of having to face and understand an obstacle in order to stop and think. I connect the educational use of aporia with a form of the uncanny, where the operation of ignorance is not blank, but is instead a weighted ignorance, aware of something that lingers in an uncomfortable state that wavers between familiar and unfamiliar. I contend that vertigo is a state of discomfort that is aware of this fearful familiarity that has been repressed. I suggest in conclusion that the initial suspicions attending the uncanny and the vertiginous responsibility of accounting for one's place in the world are useful antidotes to the problems attending educational comfort.

To illustrate the dynamics of comfort, the uncanny, and vertigo, I examine contemporary writings on feminism, race, and education. Jane Roland Martin argues that schools ought to reflect more of the domestic, while Bernice Johnson Reagon and Minnie Bruce Pratt strongly link critical reflection and political action with a move away from the desire to have a comfortable home, a move toward struggles and relations with others. I want to support this latter move away from caring, not because theorists are incorrect when they assert that we ought to care, but because their message too easily traps us into a therapeutic, one-on-one caring relationship with students. This domestic relation impedes our obligation to push students (and ourselves) out into the responsibility of relations with others in ways that are unlikely to lead to domestic and cozy comfort. I do not mean this as a fully heartless response to dynamics of power, subjectivity, and responsibility, but I want to account for the central role the inequalities of the world have in maintaining home as a place apart and a place of studied ignorance.[2]

In a time when the version of home in education all too often collapses into explanations of student attitude based on their "family background," when students become the objects of care through therapeutic forms of education including calls for empathy and connection, home is a problematic concept as yet to be fully taken apart. This is especially problematic as social inequality collapses into discourses of trauma, and when conservative as well as progressive voices call for home schooling. Each of these moves has in common a representation of learning as comfort, an understanding of relations with others as psychologically integrating. Instead education ought to cultivate alienation and an alienated subjectivity.[3] The aporia, the uncanny, and the unsettling are the very reason we engage in education, and we ought to embrace the discomforts of obstacles and understand our engagements with the world and others as fraught with difficulty. Rather than shying away from these difficulties, they should find a central place in education that cultivates an appreciation for the discomforts of the world over the purported comforts of home.

Domesticating Education

In contrast with the notion of education as necessarily discomforting, some recent theorists have argued that education might be made more socially responsible—more worldly—by making it more homelike. As Jane Roland Martin advocates education for domestic tranquility, she pushes us to think "about the kind of home we want our nation to be and the kind of family we want its inhabitants to be."[4] In her book-length work, *The Schoolhome*,[5] and in other versions of what I will refer to as therapeutic multiculturalism, education is linked also with the development of comfort in the world. These works advocate for schools to more closely resemble the home cultures of all students, just as they have always purportedly resembled the home culture of white middle-class students. What all of these versions of education have in common is the notion that learning ought to be comforting, that situations in which students and teachers confront and interrogate one another and new ideas ought not to be so contentious that students prefer to retreat to the place of home. But the solutions suggested in these calls for homelike versions of schools and familylike versions of social space neglect an important distinction: Public space is not private space (and I would argue, following Catherine MacKinnon, neither is private space so private for women, or for other groups). To return public school to the space of family comfort, of course, presupposes that families are comfortable places. Martin is well aware that the domestic sphere as currently constituted is not an ideal model, recounting the pervasiveness of domestic violence in what currently serves as the domestic sphere.[6] She is not advocating, of course, for the continuation of current domestic problems but for the best form of the domestic. Martin argues that we give little attention to what we take to be our natural relations of home, and too much attention to cultivating the ability of students to enter the public. As such, she argues, the domestic becomes something "we must learn to go beyond."[7] She argues against an education that concentrates on the civic virtues of citizenship and patriotism, contending that education ought to cultivate "a commitment to safety—bodily and psychological integrity."[8] I think the desire for safety maintains social relationships of inequality and want to instead argue that the very contentiousness of public (and private) spaces is eroded and elided when models of education that seek to soothe students overwhelm models of education that seek to disturb them. I strongly disagree, then, with Martin's assertion that "we reclaim the civic or public realm as a domestic domain"[9] even if this task is undertaken to bring tranquility to the domestic. Tranquility is too close to an easy status quo. Further, the challenges facing anti-bias education are not so easily solved, and cultivating our students' capacities to grapple with difficult relations remains our greatest challenge.

Stunning Ignorance

The process of education confronts the rootedness of home with the unmooring of relations of others; the purpose of liberal education is touted as that which removes students from a world "lapped round with locality."[10] While liberal education has been criticized for installing a particular version of the world that too closely resembles the "home" of some students, it is worth considering the importance of educational projects that attempt to move majority students out of the home that may have maintained their complacent ignorance. Minority students already experience this wrench away from comfort, and already know that they must know at least two worlds in order to negotiate schooling. My point is not to magnify their discomfort but to help to show how the experience of reorienting oneself in a variety of contexts can be of educational use. Honing the critical possibilities of this process can help both minority students who already engage in reorientation as a matter of course, and it can help majority students who haven't felt the need to reorient themselves or who don't experience shifts in context that stun them into reconsideration of their knowledge and practices.

Recentering "aporia" in education may be one way to overcome the "nonengagement" of majority students and to illuminate the knowledge-making abilities of minority students. Rather than focusing on what majority students know, centralizing aporia would move the educational project to focus on what they don't know. The task becomes to stun them with their own socially acceptable ignorance. This process recapitulates Socrates' account of the difficulties of learning. Socrates describes the ability to be open to learning in physically uncomfortable and unsettling terms: turning one's head toward knowledge—or, as Meno describes his experience of Socrates' questioning, being stung by a stingray and numbed in the pursuit of knowledge.[11] To stimulate these difficulties, rather than avert them, Socrates sorts through these obstacles to knowledge with interlocutors with whom he disagrees. In other words, he does not shy away from people who most doubt and disparage him, nor does he shy away from people whose practices he abhors. This, to a certain extent, might encourage a view of knowledge as that which requires discussion, dispute, and adversity. Socrates views his place in the world as necessarily contentious. Certainly his refusal to leave Athens and the polis, even when it meant his death, indicates his willingness to remain in conflict rather than seek safety. The polis was of course not ideal; certainly its existence depended on the exploitation of others: slaves, women, non-Greeks. Further, it is plausible to interpret Socrates' turn to knowledge from the otherworld as indicating that knowledge is discovered, not created. But for the purposes of this examination of the educational use of aporia, my focus is on the capacity to grapple with the disabling potential of one's purported "knowledge" in order to get around what is actually one's ignorance.

As much as obstacles pull the learner into a realization of ignorance, the aporia is filled, eventually, by what the learner already knew in the otherworld. Whether one views this as the capacity to learn that preexists the particular use to which it is put or the social (or spiritual) ground on which all knowledge rests, Socrates indicates that the learner, even in the deepest perplexity, still has familiarity with the knowledge he or she does not know. This process requires, most importantly, the recognition of the contours of ignorance that structure the mistaken presumption of knowledge. So the first aid that Socrates provides for antiracist education is the reminder that ignorance is a necessary starting point, but that ignorance is not empty. Ignorance is the workings of a solipsism that is unable to see that the world may be understood differently by others. When that solipsism confronts itself and sees itself as an obstacle, there is potential for getting beyond the stalled misrecognition of the world. Overcoming the aporia of this solipsism is the realization of having forgotten a problem that needs to be solved because of overconfidence in existing knowledge. But confronting the aporia does not mean that one necessarily stays stunned, it means that one begins to recognize that the capacity to be stunned signifies that something more is required. Thus, the aporia that numbs Meno is the occasion for examining how he had forgotten his capacity to learn the knowledge that he already "knows."[12] For students engaged in antiracist education, developing the capacity to interrogate their "stunning ignorance" means, first of all, recognizing when their confidence in their knowledge and place in the world disables them from viewing it from other perspectives.

But it is not always possible to overcome aporia, nor would it always be right to do so. Part of the problem of living in a position of dominance is the confidence in the ability to know, to always be able to sort out differences of opinion or to fully understand everything in the world. Aporia can be a reminder that some things are beyond the reach of assimilable knowledge and understanding. For learners whose solipsism has disabled them, recognition of the boundaries their place in the world puts on the reach of their knowledge may also be a helpful reminder of the limits of knowledge and the intransigence of ignorance. But at the very least, a suspicion that one does not know as much as one thinks one knows allows one to remain more open to the possibility of difficult relations. Further, a suspicion about one's ignorance can be a motivation to form relations that keep one grappling with one's understanding of the world.

Uncanny Resemblance

Part of the reason majority students (and instructors) are reluctant to engage with the aporia of their own ignorance is a lurking or repressed full understanding of the moral implications of the unjust place they occupy in the world. While centralizing the process of recognizing, confronting, and maintaining aporia are important to antiracist education, attention to the uncanny is a further requirement. The uncanny can help to illuminate the reluctance to push beyond what seems to be innocent ignorance. In his discussion of the uncanny, Freud examines how the dynamics of repression undergird what is familiar with a discomforting echo of what is strange, and vice versa. While the focus of his essay is on the techniques of literature that produce the feeling of the uncanny, his observations provide a helpful parallel to one of the central difficulties of antiracist education: the discomfort of white students who simultaneously know enough about race relations to know why they should be uncomfortable in such discussions and who also claim ignorance about race relations. In other words, like the examples Freud uses to explain the particular unsettling quality of the uncanny, these students have a familiarity with problems they have in some way either actively repressed or been encouraged by social norms to ignore. Their repression is, in my view, less of a psychological dynamic than a reflection of the general social tendency to ignore difficult topics. Students' frequent participation in such a form of "social repression," shows that they do know "something familiar which has been repressed" about race.[13]

Highlighting the "uncanny" aspects of race relations may be a helpful pedagogical way to avoid the dogmatism of "just don't be racist" because it calls on students to make an unsettling problem of their race-related fear and familiarity. Like the uncanny, this active form of antiracist problem posing might create an uncertainty in students. Borrowing from Freud, the uncanny might be said to create uncertainty "in such a way that [their] attention is not focused directly upon [their] uncertainty, so that [they] may not be led to go into the matter and clear it up immediately."[14]

There is promise in the uncanny destabilizing the familiar and the strange into mutually constitutive categories. It is promising in terms of anti-bias pedagogy, in terms of a pedagogy reliant on riddles and puzzles that require background knowledge, but also one that should simultaneously trouble the very background that enables such knowledge.

Mistaking Cliché for Student Voice

All too often discussions about student voice devolve into calls for opening spaces for them to speak what they already know. This inevitably leads us into the sterile problem Dewey argued against: raw experience is not necessarily experience that is educational. This raw experience, where students give voice to what they knew prior to engaging with others, is self-centered, less interested in further association than in concretizing its own place. Thus, this centering of discomfort is particularly critical for teaching students antiracism. As students recall what they know from home, they rely on the comforts of dinner table conversations, the very conversations they feel compelled to repeat uncritically and nearly compulsively as they are faced with a world unfamiliar to them. When students, for example, recount their first interaction with a black person as a moment where they looked up from their yard or from their place on their mother's lap and screamed at the sight of an unfamiliar hue, they are recounting precisely why education ought not to be home. Home is where the scream is inculcated and expected, because of a lack of the unfamiliar. Education is where the scream ought to be problematized, where what one had previously thought one did not need to know pushes one into a relation with this self-alienating relationship. I contend that these relationships are self-alienating because one's definition of oneself is maintained through the expectation that the world is a familiar place, that one will not encounter startling or ignored difference.

Families and churches remain the most starkly segregated institutions in our society. Whether or not they manage it in practice, families are supposed to provide for affective support and warm encouragement. Meeting others with whom one is unfamiliar, in contrast, is a potentially aporia-generating experience. Facing the responsibility for race relations, particularly for students who have never considered race relations a problem, ought to generate the numbing effect Meno described. The experience ought not to send them into a comfortable exchange of stories, but should push them into a painful, critical reexamination of their active ignorance about difference. This active form of ignorance is what most troubles me about the desire to make antiracist education or any education comfortable. Many of us have taken great feats of subtle strategy to maintain our ability to be comfortable in the world in ways that directly impede the comforts of others. That this form of ignorance directly involves our actively ignoring the very lack of knowledge that would otherwise stun us— preferably into action against that which we guard ourselves against knowing— means that we are fully complicit even when blissfully unaware. While I am not arguing that we send our white, or other majority, students into paroxysms of liberal guilt, I am certain that they ought not to require carefully nurtured prodding into concerns about justice.

Family as the Cause of Racism, Autobiography as the Cure

It might reasonably be argued at this point that Roland Martin's call for the "3 Cs of care, concern, and connection" in her plan for domestic education and Noddings's call for caring in schools are useful antidotes to the apparent trauma of racism. I want to steer us far away from the discourse of racism as the result of individual family-based trauma. One particularly pernicious example, popular in antiracist curricula, is the film *The Color of Fear*, in which a male mixed-race encounter group thrashes out race relations over the course of a weekend at what appears to be a California spa or convention center. As they recount stories of race relations, one white man increasingly becomes the center of their attention as they root through his past to find the kernel of truth that mobilized his racism. This therapeutic setting enables the classic domestic explanation: His father abused him. The problem of race is then the problem of his family, and while the family writ large stands in for the wounded white man's race relations, it is a return to family dynamics that uncovers where the therapeutic cure for his racism lies. We find the same sort of call for domestic healing of racism whenever exhausted teachers and professors turn away from curricular ways to address racism and turn back to the family. As one professor recently put it at a conference on hate crimes at the university, "What can we do when these students come from families whose socio-economic status makes their racism possible, even necessary?" That the particular university in question was unable to recruit or retain students of color at a rate of more than 5 percent clearly points to institutional responsibility, not family failings.

We need to recognize the discourse of family-based racism, where racism is "bred in the bone," as an avoidance of discussions of social forces and institutions that require racism. The turn toward domestic or psychological causes of racism individualizes broad social problems and installs a subjectivity doggedly unable to leave home and get to school. This, it seems to me, is precisely the problem with therapeutic-domestic education. Students do not need the comforts of home or home remedies, they need to get out and mingle with others beyond their knowing and begin to understand the world as a place in which they are not meant to feel the arrogance of comfort.

To avoid this arrogance of comfort, we need to sidestep what seems to be an all too common feature of diversity education: the telling of the personal story as if the subject of the story were disconnected from relations of identity. We should not encourage the telling of students' selves without adequately interrogating what a self or subject is, and how the very constitution of subjectivity is part of a discourse of authenticity and authority underwriting racism, as well as other forms of bias. In other words, we should not encourage students to concretize their subjectivity without adequately attending to historical contingency and power relations subtending claims to know oneself. Further, stories often neglect the hidden relationships among other subjectivities and thus maintain ignorance of how, for instance, white racial or ethnic identity is constructed and understood in relation to nonwhite identities. Stories that stand side by side to illustrate that we're all different neglect to show that, whether we acknowledge it or not, we're all related in the terms we use. We are related inasmuch as we use each other to form concretized senses of our own identities.

By now I have been to at least half a dozen diversity training sessions where participants were invited to each get up on a stool and tell their family story. One person might come from a working-class Italian background, another from a middle-class African American background, and so on. The impetus behind this exercise is partially to remind all people that their identities are marked because people in the majority categories may too often consider themselves the universal subject. In the end, the objective always seems to be that we all have complicated lives and would do well to realize that of each other. While this is doubtless a start, understanding that some of us complicate the lives of others differently would help to raise the relational stakes of this exercise. Diversity workshop participants are encouraged to take seriously the role of social positioning in the constitution of their subjectivity, but this process tends to reinstall uninterrogated identity categories and neglect the power relations between identity categories. By conflating all identity as difference, then, we open the possibility that students will assert that being German is necessarily equivalent to being Latina. All difference becomes exchangeable without an understanding of social and political forces; all differences are identified as having (false) family resemblances and thus bring students into what they take as closer understandings of themselves and others.[15]

But here are some stories that don't fit well together. A class discussion of women's sexuality was taken over by the two men in class, who spent the greater portion of the discussion both explaining their own difficulties with women and castigating women in the class for not chiming in with their own stories. Despite numerous attempts to steer these men away from talking, including a long discussion on why some people taking up discussion time meant that other people wouldn't be talking nor would be particularly inclined to share intimate details, nothing stopped the incessant storytelling of the men. We broke into small groups, and most groups discussed why they weren't going to participate, given that the men whose talking had taken up all the airspace seemed, much too paradoxically, to want the women to talk. As a few women pointed out later, they were hardly going to help these boorish men understand women's sexuality, given that they couldn't understand how to listen in the first place. Now, clearly part of this story is also my ineptitude as an instructor, but another part is that the women read the context of story sharing as one in which it really didn't matter what they said and so there was no point in saying it. Add that to the detail that the discussion was about the "myth of the vaginal orgasm" and the general cultural ignorance of the clitoris and one can see that the men were likely talking to cover their discomfort of the topic and shift that discomfort onto the women in class. The moral of this story about stories is not that everyone should have talked and understood their relationality, although that certainly would have been an improvement. Instead, the difficulty of speaking and even entering into a relationship was highlighted for the women, who had long experience with such things but nonetheless made the incident a central part of their experience of the class. That they had so starkly been reminded of how much men control conversations and sexual knowledge meant that they were able to share an experience with one another and rethink the degree to which they wished to establish classroom relations across the gender divide. They clearly recognized the double bind: To insist on a classroom relationship with the men meant continuing to give the men attention; to ignore a classroom relationship with the men meant continuing to allow them to speak unchallenged. And I was left with numerous office hours trying to explain that the class was not jelling because the men were opting out of recognizing their role as obstacle to the formation of a difficult relationship, while the men continued to assert that it was the women who were opting out.

Another difficult series of stories that wouldn't sit comfortably side by side started with the topic of racial segregation but moved to gay rights. White students initially discussed what they hoped would have been their active response against racial segregation, but more than a few were deeply concerned that they would have accepted the dominant norms. We were talking about how the larger issues of racism and other forms of bias structure social interactions and thus actively limit the spaces in which relations across difference can even happen. While mulling the historical example of legalized segregation, a black student suggested that a white person moving to the back of the bus wouldn't help the situation because he or she was then taking up one of the few seats a person of color could legally occupy. A student of color pointed out that even having shared the space, a white person couldn't fully understand what it meant to be the person who had to sit there and who had to understand the full ramifications across the range of social, political, and economic meanings of sitting there. Ultimately the problem the class grappled with was that one can potentially have a relationship across difference and still be faced with a great divide. Many students had been advocating empathy as a way to bridge the divide but were beginning to be moved away from their belief that they could ever feel what another person felt. In short, they were beginning to see that relation does not necessarily imply a similar viewpoint but rather an active decision to cross a divide that is maintained through activity that looks like passivity.

As the class started to try to ferret out where they were actively passively allowing divides to be maintained, a lesbian student pointed out that straight people passively decide to go about their lives, all the time ignoring the differences between their lives and the lives of sexual minority people all around them. She pointed out that she had been to multiple weddings, given away multiple small kitchen appliances, but no one had ever noticed that she had been with her female partner for many years. There wasn't an equivalence to their relationship and heterosexual relationships; there wasn't an easily socially sanctioned way to celebrate their relationship, nor was there even an indication from heterosexual friends that they realized that marriage was a segregated institution. Classmates who had imagined themselves perhaps attempting to ride in the back of the bus objected that they could hardly be expected to give up having families because the law prevented gay and lesbian couples from marrying. A few confusedly asked if it weren't true that many places allowed gay marriage and were surprised to find that rumors of gay marriage's legality were greatly exaggerated. All students in class said that they had gay friends, lesbian relatives, or at least some firsthand experience with a person who was not heterosexual. None of them had noticed or been particularly troubled that the major life cycle events and rituals they had been to had excluded celebrations of same sex couples.

So they at once knew gay people as friends or relatives, but didn't notice their absence from the center of social ritual or think about the further implications of that absence (in terms of hospital visitation, adoption, property, simple social recognition). But they all knew that there was a similarity between gay and straight relationships, so at once the resemblance was clear, but unmarked by actual practices like ceremonies. Further, the differences between gay and straight relationships were somehow not recognizable because they simply did not see the exclusions visited on gay couples. As one student said, having prided herself on not seeing the difference between gays and straights, it was difficult to consider that there were, in fact, differences. She said it was particularly hard to realize that her heterosexuality insisted on and maintained those differences through social institutions but that her sense of herself as "kind of progressive" depended on her saying that there weren't differences. In other words, her comfort with herself as social progressive wound up being part of what discouraged her from considering difference as something that needed to be maintained at the forefront of discussions of bias.

Moving out of the Self, out of Identity, and into a Vertigo of Action

Bernice Johnson Reagon has argued that this sense of comfort is not the point of a political agenda that addresses racism through coalition politics. As she puts it:

> Coalition work is not work done in your home. Coalition work has to be done in the streets. And it is some of the most dangerous work you can do. And you shouldn't look for comfort. Some people will come to a coalition and rate the success of the coalition on whether or not they feel good when they get there. They're not looking for a coalition, they're looking for a home. They're looking for a bottle with some milk in it and a nipple, which does not happen in a coalition. You don't get a lot of food in a coalition. In a coalition you have to give, and it is different from your home. You can't stay there all the time.[16]

Reagon clearly shows the problems of turning diversity and antiracist education into a comfortable endeavor, as she argues that the recognition of similarity and the need to be comfortable with similarity keeps people in "little barred rooms."[17] Whether these rooms are made up of people of particular identity group similarities or perceived similarities is unimportant: After a time they become exclusionary.

The difficulties of separation and association are clear, as Minnie Bruce Pratt recounts the pull and the impossibility of home and firm boundaries on identity in her essay "Identity: Skin Blood Heart." For Pratt, the voices of black men in her neighborhood recall her home and at the same time remind her that home is based on exclusion:

> I think how I just want to feel at home, where people know me; instead I remember, when I meet Mr. Boone, that home was a place of forced subservience, and I know that my wish is that of an adult wanting to stay a child: to be known by others, but to know nothing, to feel no responsibility.[18]

Rather than staying in the place of nostalgia and comfort, Pratt's experience becomes "fraught, for me, with the history of race and sex and class; as I walk I have a constant interior discussion with myself, question how I acknowledge the presence of another, what I know or don't know about them, and what it means how they acknowledge me."[19] Her very actions of reflection and recounting the impossibility of writing a stable autobiography or returning to the nostalgia of home make home and self themselves impossible. That is, by engaging in this kind of work, she is unable to go home, as home is a place where these questions would have been unacceptable. She recounts her father's attempt, when she was young, to introduce her to his view of the world by climbing to the top of the courthouse, and tells of her failure to make that climb and have that view. But she is also well aware that her place in the world as a white woman makes that view not something given up by conscience but rather one that remains even in her attempts to actively not have it. As she engages in her work, she effaces her own particular viewpoint: "I am struggling now to speak, but not out of any role of ought-to; I ask that you try not to place me in that role."[20] She explains, "I began when I jumped from my edge and outside myself."[21]

She describes the Greensboro massacre, where Klansmen killed Communist activists demonstrating against racism, as a turning point in her thinking: What else had these Klansmen done to protect white womanhood? Pratt's historical examination of the production of white womanhood and the attendant ills visited on black men and women in its name produced in her "a kind of vertigo: a sensation of my body having no fixed place to be."[22] At one level, this is good, second-wave autobiography whose intent is to explain an authentic experience as a political starting point. But at another level, Pratt wants her own experience not to stand for itself but to encourage the uncomfortable process of her audience's tracing their own positioning in vectors of race, class, sexuality, and power. Like the numbing process of the aporia and the unsettling experience of the uncanny, the point is not the series of events leading to vertigo, but what one does with the vertiginous feeling of losing one's place and with the impossibility of reinstalling comfort as an antidote. Engaging in tracing the space of the uncanny requires the unsettling of one's place in the world and one's place in defining what one takes to be uncanny. But for Pratt, the experience of vertigo is a constant reminder of the work that needs to be done, the relationships that need to be formed, and the constant trouble that one's social position brings to any relation or project. She offers a clear reminder that one does not transcend one's position by engaging in relations with others, but rather that social position continues to drag on possibilities for relations. Still, the only option is to relate, not to retreat into the comfort of one's troubling home.

Hate Crimes, Families, and Caring

At a recent conference on the role of the university in preventing hate crimes such as those that occurred a few summers ago in the Midwest by an Indiana University student, Eva Cherniavsky criticized the affective and family-based response from the dean of students at Indiana University.[23] Faced with explaining how his university intended to address the shooting daths, he pointed to a program where individuals of different races, himself included, get together, barbecue, meet each other's families and, in the end, become like family themselves: the all too classic refrain resounding through slavery and servitude.

Cherniavsky derided this tactic as reinstalling the embattled white masculinity, via the pater familias, behind the hate crime itself.[24] To encourage educators and students to view their relationships as revisiting family relations may also revisit a pesky gender binary that makes education into a helping profession. No doubt many of us, particularly women faculty, have been warned against baking or giving out our home phone numbers, with the caution that students will need to be reminded that "you are not their mother." In reference to the same hate crime, Stephanie Foote contended that we ought to refuse to engage in the kind of care that a comforting role in education typifies. Instead she advocates dealing with the problems of hate crime and bias in general as structural problems, not problems to be dealt with by what she calls "therapeutic teaching."[25] Too often the therapeutic gesture is directed at the dominant persons trying to deal with the difficult ethical problems that attend their social position. To address the feelings of difficulty without dealing with the power inequities that create those feelings misses the point of education: the formation of difficult relations, not to comfort those involved but to grapple with and address the structuring problems.

Rather than work to make education about difficult issues easier, we do better to maintain anti-bias education as unsettling but necessarily relational. These processes, like all engagements with learning what we find difficult, are uncomfortable. Discussions around topics like racism that have so long been the purview of active, constant ignorance, in the clearest sense of ignoring what is palpably present, are uncomfortable precisely because so much effort has gone into ignoring them. To bring anti-bias education into a comforting environment, then, misses the point. If the world is home because it was ensured that it was not someone else's, we must give up home in order to engage in difficult relations.

Notes

1. Rudolfo Chavez Chavez and James O'Donnell, eds.,"Introduction," *Speaking the Unpleasant: The Politics of (Non) Engagement in the Multicultural Education Terrain* (Albany, NY: SUNY Press, 1998), 2.
2. See also Ann Diller's presidential address to the Philosophy of Education Society, "Facing the Torpedo Fish: Becoming a Philosopher of One's Own Education," *Philosophy of Education 1998*, ed. Steve Tozer (Urbana, IL: Philosophy of Education Society, 1999): 1–9.
3. I see this as connected to Natasha Levinson's work on "belatedness." See Levinson's "Teaching in the Midst of Belatedness: The Paradox of Natality in Hannah Arendt's Educational Thought," *Educational Theory* 47, no. 4 (Fall 1997): 441.

4. Jane Roland Martin, "Education for Domestic Tranquility," in *Critical Conversations in Philosophy of Education*, ed. Wendy Kohli (New York: Routledge, 1995), 47.

5. Jane Roland Martin, *The Schoolhome: Rethinking Schools for Changing Families* (Cambridge, MA: Harvard University Press, 1992).

6. Martin, "Education for Domestic Tranquility," 48.

7. Martin, "Education for Domestic Tranquility," 52.

8. Martin, "Education for Domestic Tranquility," 53.

9. Martin, "Education for Domestic Tranquility," 49.

10. Michael Oakeshott, *The Voice of Liberal Learning* (New Haven, CN: Yale University Press, 1989).

11. Other philosophers have also discussed the discomfort of learning—Lyotard contending that education is terror, Gadamer contending that we only think when we are confused or confounded—all versions of learning well in keeping with Meno's reaction to Socrates.

12. That this process occurs through Socrates' dialogue with Meno's slave may underscore the inevitable pull of knowledge beyond the consent of the one being pulled, but it also indicates the different experiences of knowledge based on social position. For Meno, the dialogue is philosophically interesting, for the slave, who knows?

13. Sigmund Freud, Freud, Sigmund, "The 'Uncanny,'" in *The Standard Edition of the Complete Psychological Works of Sigmund Freud*, vol. 17, trans. and ed. James Strachey (London: Hogarth Press, 1955), 247.

14. Freud, "The Uncanny," 227.

15. Indeed, a closer examination of Wittgenstein's version of "family resemblances" might be helpful here in separating and untangling the different meanings and positions of a variety of subjectivities, not all of whom may, in the end, share a family resemblance.

16. Bernice Johnson Reagon, "Coalition Politics: Turning the Century," in *Home Girls: A Black Feminist Anthology*, ed. Barbara Smith (New York: Kitchen Table: Women of Color Press, 1983), 359.

17. Reagon, "Coalition Politics," 358.

18. Minnie Bruce Pratt, "Identity: Skin Blood Heart," in *Yours in Struggle: Three Feminist Perspectives on Anti-Semitism and Racism*, ed. Elly Bulkin, Minnie Bruce Pratt, and Barbara Smith (Brooklyn: Long Haul Press, 1984), 12.

19. Pratt, "Identity: Skin Blood Heart," 12.

20. Pratt, "Identity: Skin Blood Heart," 15.

21. Pratt, "Identity: Skin Blood Heart," 19.

22. Pratt, "Identity: Skin Blood Heart," 35.

23. In the summer of 1999, a white neo-Nazi Indiana University student went on a hate-driven shooting spree, killing two people of color and wounding a number of others before killing himself during a police chase.

24. Eva Cherniavsky, "Ethnic Cleansing at the University," *American Studies Roundtable*, Indiana University at Bloomington, September 30, 1999.

25. Stephanie Foote, "The Working Conditions of Ethical Teaching," *Concerns: A Journal of the MLA Women's Caucus*, 25 no. 1 (Spring 2000): 33-53. Another panelist, in contrast, called for better relations with the police and FBI, as they bring comfort (as an audience member cat-called, "to white people").

PART 3

KNOWLEDGE, CURRICULUM, AND RELATION

KNOWING IS RESPONSE-ABLE RELATION

Barbara S. Stengel

Knowing is response-able relation. If this thesis is correct—if this is something that I know—then it does us no good to proceed in the usual scholarly way, defining terms and defending claims. Such an effort would simply catalog what I know; it would not enable you to come to know what you do not know now. Let me try another tack, one more congruent with my thesis.

Right Answers and Right Relations

When my daughter Emily was five, she took an oral Wechsler IQ test. I sat quietly across the room as she pondered each of the psychologist's questions and answered with no fear and with occasional relish. She was a study in thoughtfulness. At one point, the psychologist asked her to name two differences between a car and a bike. She hesitated just a moment before saying, "If you take a car, you'll get there faster." The psychologist accepted that answer and prompted her for a second response. Emily looked puzzled and said, "There aren't any others." It was the psychologist's turn to look puzzled. He suggested that she think about it a bit more. She sat quite composed for perhaps a minute and then quietly repeated her response. The psychologist noted her inability to answer and proceeded to the next question.

Three days later, in the car returning from an errand, Emily asked, "Mom, what was the answer to that question about the car and the bike?" I replied that cars have four wheels and bikes have two. She told me that that could not be right because bikes with training wheels had four wheels. So I tried again. I told her that cars have roofs and bikes don't. She piped back that that wasn't it, that we were riding in a convertible without a roof, and anyway, the surrey bike we rode at the beach the previous week did have a roof. Fair enough, I thought, and then I took my best shot. I told my daughter that cars had engines and bikes didn't. She looked directly at me and said, seeming a little surprised at my ignorance, "Well, you know, Mom, if you really think about it, on a bike, your feet on the pedals *are* the engine." At that point, I admitted defeat and offered no other response. I was cowed into silence by a mind more facile than my own. In truth, I was delighted to realize that Emily's mind worked so richly and well, and a bit chastened to recognize the extent to which my own thinking had been constrained by conventional categories. That is not the end of this story, however.

Six years later, I was involved in a conversation with another educator in which this story about Emily's IQ test experience came up. Emily overheard. She asked me to repeat the story. I told her about the question on the IQ test and about her response during the test session, and mentioned but did not describe our later discussion of engines and so on. She responded, "Oh, I was so dumb then." I asked her what her answer to that question would be were she asked today. She rattled off the same differences that I had once offered to her. The richness of her thinking had disappeared while her IQ had apparently—and ironically—increased! What had happened to Emily in the years between five and eleven? How did she come to know these differences between a car and a bike? And why did she now dismiss her earlier answers as "dumb"? I believe that the changes in Emily's understanding can be explained by looking at the explicitly educational relations in her life at those two times.

In the years preceding her sixth birthday, Emily spent much of her time (at least half of every day) with one caretaker, Anna, whom most would describe as "uneducated" but whose openness, sense of wonder, and spirit of adventure would easily have grounded Emily's expansive thinking about cars and bikes. Anna was sixty and a physically active grandmother when Emily was born. She began to care for Emily within weeks of her birth, and from the start, shared her own active approach to the world. By the time Emily could toddle, they would set out in mid-morning as the sun warmed the world and be gone for a couple of hours, stopping at the park or at the playground or at the bus stop or any other place that caught their fancy. As they walked, they talked to each other and to those they encountered. At home, they played games and read books and asked and answered questions, usually with both Anna and Emily on the floor.

When not with Anna, Emily spent time in a preschool where play and playfulness were the only real rules, and in a household where everybody's ideas, ideas of all kinds, were entertained openly and taken seriously. In both cases and places, relationships with others (teachers and family members) were the vessels that conveyed understanding marked by openness.

By the time she was in sixth grade, Emily was spending her days in a typical school environment where relations with teachers were subordinated to the subject matter to be learned and where she was encouraged to evaluate herself with reference to a particular brand of academic performance. I do not mean to suggest that her teachers were unkind or inconsiderate. Most were quite personable and friendly. Nor do I mean to suggest that they were ineffective. Perhaps the point is that they *were* effective, that they focused (and succeeded in focusing Emily) on the acquisition of "knowledge," of separable subject matters—sets of facts and skills—that could be itemized, codified, and assessed. Knowing was no longer a function of mutual relationships of inquiry and openness; rather, knowing was constituted as a function of relationships that can be categorized as hierarchical, disciplined, and authoritative. This eager-to-please, preadolescent girl learned only too well that the best answer was the answer the teacher expected, that those who did not identify the "right" answer were "dumb."

While home was still a place where divergent thinking was welcome, Emily was spending more time away from home—at basketball practice where divergent thinking was forbidden and with friends who, as Emily did, measured their march to maturity largely in terms of their adherence to the conventional standards of their peer culture. School and community conspired to construct a view of knowledge as given rather than transacted. While something was gained, something significant was lost. In contrast to her later, school-based orientation to knowledge, Emily's first understanding of the differences between a car and a bike was framed by her primary, explicitly educational relations. Emily's "right relation" with Anna, a relation of mutual engagement, enabled a richly observant understanding of her world; her constrained, if still caring, relations with teachers in school resulted in a narrowed focus on the "right answer." The point to be made here is not that her relation with Anna is better than her relations with her teachers. The point is more basic: In the domain of education (within the horizon of educational intentions), knowing is response-able relation. Relation inevitably yields knowledge of a certain quality, knowledge that then shapes the possibility of response-in-relation.

"Knowledge" under Suspicion

Before explicating two other examples from Emily's education, let me talk more about my central claim. It is that knowledge is response-able relation. This has a dual meaning: (1) that knowing arises not merely as a function of an individual consciousness at work but as a by-product of the interaction, the relations, between and among persons in particular contexts, and (2) that to know, to have knowledge, is, in the first place, to (be able to) respond to others in particular circumstances. As an educator, I am interested in the linkage among learning, knowledge, and teaching as a relational activity. Both traditional and contemporary educational activity and theory tend to begin with a view of knowledge, marry that view of knowledge to a learning theory, and then cash that out into some recommended set of teacher-student relations.

For example, the contemporary standards initiatives in the United States focus on knowledge as previously established facts and useful (typically cognitive) skills. These initiatives complement that view with a learning theory that might best be described as information processing. Relations between teachers and students are marked, then, by control, expertise, authority, and surveillance, though within these limits, relations may also be affectionate and sensitive.

In an alternative example, there is the educator who holds hope for a "structure of the disciplines" approach, who views knowledge as understanding born of inquiry. When yoked to a vision of the learner as actively making meaning, a prescription for teacher as the students' guide emerges. The guide challenges *and* supports. Neither of these approaches seem adequate, though I much prefer the latter to the former. They are inadequate not because of the specific relations they recommend but for two more basic reasons: (1) both the traditional and the inquiry-based view privilege the stance of the apparently powerful, of the expert/teacher, without recognition of the power of the student; and (2) both rely on a fundamentally instrumental approach to a fundamentally relational activity. For both political and logical reasons, it seems worthwhile to reverse the equation, to begin with relation rather than with knowledge. What if educators like me began their work with a focus on the relation, the interaction, between and among teachers and students? What view(s) of knowledge and knowing would follow from that starting point? The question itself is simply stated, but imagining an answer is devilishly difficult. Our conceptual apparatus seems preset to start with knowledge as the given and to view relation as derivative.

It is precisely because of the difficulty of the question and the nature of my answer that I ground my musings in some concrete example of educational experience. As exemplified above, I use my own daughter's education for two reasons. First, I have been a close and never disinterested observer of Emily's formal education from the start. In fact, of course, I have been a participant observer, meeting with teachers, helping with homework, encouraging interest and effort, chaperoning activities, cheering her on at chorus recitals and athletic events. Hers is an education I already experience relationally in a way I doubt is true even for my own.

Second, Emily's experience of formal education is, by most measures, a good experience. She has attended what most would describe as good small schools, schools with "good kids" and a strong sense of community and family support. Her schools have had adequate resources, and she has encountered competent teachers. Emily herself has been a successful student, achieving good grades and good scores on annual achievement tests. Despite this "goodness," I am acutely aware that Emily's formal education is not educative. She, like so many adolescents, cares little for the substance of her schooling. Her school knowledge does not (apparently) move her. In fact, she reports interest in almost nothing that occurs in school except social interactions. And even there, she reports that kids don't seem to treat each other very well. How could this be? How could a bright and responsible child in an apparently good school be so disengaged? The point here is not that Emily is special; it's that she really isn't. She has it about as good as it gets in contemporary schooling. I believe that the key to understanding Emily's lack of engagement is the problem outlined above: that her educators are beginning with a view of knowledge (typically a view of knowledge as proposition and performance) and determining relations that fit that view, rather than beginning with the fact of teacher-student relation and imagining the knowledge that issues from those relations and that in turn enables and enacts knowing as response in richer and/or new relations.

What counts as knowledge is precisely what is at stake in this essay. The encyclopedic understanding of knowledge as the codification of all that humans understand and can do is placed under suspicion. The notion that this understanding—in its modern iteration of academic standards—is the starting place for educational efforts is put aside in favor of a focus on relation. Views that catalog facts and skills under the rubric of knowledge are valuable but as tertiary analytic reconstructions of the residue of human experience. They are useful *after the fact* because they allow one to compare and confirm one's own achieved understanding against the understandings achieved by others. However, no such catalog can ground a process that is, at base, relational.

I turn back now to Emily's education with two additional examples. I introduce you to my thesis through the suggestive use of these narratives. As you come to be acquainted with her and her stories through me, you may also come to recognize, to know, the centrality of relation in your own educational experience.

Science as Solitary Studies

Emily hates science. She will tell you loudly and often. She didn't hate science as a youngster; she didn't hate science until she began to "study science." As a small child, she was fascinated by and unafraid of bugs and other creatures, more than willing to pick them up and try to figure them out. Her IQ test answer about the car and the bike suggests that she was well able to apply a kind of scientific inquiry to physical phenomena. When asked if she wanted to participate in the school science fair as a first grader, she responded yes enthusiastically and proceeded to complete a remarkably sophisticated study to determine the right mix of baking soda and vinegar to blow a balloon up as fully as possible. She had seen the idea depicted in a book of science fair ideas belonging to her older brother, figured out what it was about, and created a research plan not unlike the one the book recommended. Multiple trials with various amounts of baking soda and vinegar in a contraption with a balloon tightly secured to the end of a straw allowed her to conclude that more of one ingredient was good only if you used more of the other.

In second grade, she completed a naturalistic study of a single black rat snake—her Christmas present that year. She kept a journal of observations over a six-week period (which conveniently included a period in which the snake shed its skin) and reported her observations, carefully noting the significant limitation of her study, namely, that she couldn't be sure that her snake was like all other snakes. In third grade (the science fair was now mandatory, as the study of science had officially begun), she conducted an elegant inquiry into which brand of bubble gum produced the largest bubbles. She amassed samples of four brands of bubble gum, gathered a bubble-blowing board of six individuals (including both adults and children), and measured bubbles using a homemade wire device. She conducted three trials for each bubble blower for each brand of bubble gum, calculated the average size of the bubbles associated with each brand, and drew conclusions.

She continued to complete a science fair project each year as required. Each year she received no feedback except a grade from her teacher. She never won a first, second, or third place ribbon; she never received an honorable mention certificate. The projects were not discussed in school, either to plan the study, to monitor understanding of scientific inquiry, or to process the findings. For Emily, science was a solitary affair, marked by facts to be memorized and apparently pointless studies to be conducted in isolation.

While Emily seemed to enjoy her early ventures into scientific inquiry, it became a chore sometime after third grade. No "official" feedback told her whether she was successful or unsuccessful in her work. No interaction drew her and her ideas into a "scientific community." She lost the interest she had seemed to have earlier. In eighth grade, a brief moment of interest was rekindled by the nature of the study she chose. We had recently inherited a hot tub, complete with warnings that young people and people with various medical conditions should be careful in using it. As she was quite interested in using the hot tub, I suggested that she try to study the effects of hot tub sitting on a sample of young people and adults. She decided to have several hot tub parties, inviting cohorts of friends and family, both male and female, to participate. She received the appropriate human subject clearances, obtained signed releases, and went to work, measuring pre-tub, post-tub, and post-recovery pulse rate, blood pressure, and body temperature for all subjects. She used a spreadsheet to analyze the data by age and by sex. I don't recall the results, though I do recall that her data (and the approval of her physician uncle) resulted in her being given permission to use the hot tub on a regular basis. This project, the project that required her to interact with significant numbers of others in gathering data and explaining what she was up to, resulted in an honorable mention certificate—though still no comment or interaction beyond a grade from her classroom teacher. And she still hated science.

Her class grades suggested then and still suggest that she "knows" science. Marks for science in elementary school were always in the 90s. She is regularly awarded As or Bs in honors-level chemistry (now as a high school sophomore). Still, there are some signs that, despite a style of thinking that seems hospitable to scientific inquiry and apparently high levels of achievement, Emily is not learning what we would want a bright young woman to know. Her placement tests at high school admission demonstrated science knowledge that was just above average as compared to math and language scores that were significantly above average. Scores on Iowa Tests of Basic Skills taken through elementary school consistently placed her understanding of the "nature of science" in the ninth stanine and her actual knowledge of "life science," "earth and space," and "physical sciences" in the fifth and sixth stanines.

We might explain this by suggesting that despite her aptitude, Emily is simply not interested in science. But this is a descriptive, not explanatory, assessment. Why isn't she interested? She was interested as a child. And anyway, this self-reflective young lady will tell you that it's not that she's not interested; she *hates* science—or at least she hates what she has experienced as the school subject called "science." At the start of this academic year, I encountered Emily's teacher at back-to-school night. I mentioned that Emily hated science and asked if she might think about how we could address that. I thought that perhaps I might stimulate the teacher's individual interest in Emily, prompting a connection that would in turn spark understanding. The chemistry teacher, a knowledgeable and energetic woman, seemed quite shocked, indicating that Emily was a "fine student," assuming apparently that being a fine student had something to do with either interest or affection for the subject. She said she would try to address it, but perhaps this issue got lost in the shuffle of a hundred students every day. Emily still hates science.

There are a number of apparently plausible explanations for Emily's hatred of science. Perhaps her failure to win even an honorable mention ribbon for eight years in a row provided a deterrent, ultimately extinguishing her original (and admittedly rudimentary) interest in scientific observation and experimentation. Perhaps that failure was prompted by a female-socialized, peer-identified disinterest in things classed as scientific as she approached adolescence. Perhaps her elementary teachers really didn't know science themselves, and thus provided inadequate and ineffective instruction, unwittingly passing on their own discomfort with scientific inquiry and scientific knowledge. Perhaps she is resisting the expressed attitude of her high school teachers that science is the study that distinguishes the smart from the others. I believe that all of these explanations contribute to an understanding of Emily's attitude, but none are central.

The central point to be appreciated is that Emily doesn't *know* science. If she knew it, she wouldn't hate it; she would just dismiss it. She would recognize her disinterest, and allot to her study of science only that time and energy needed to maintain good grades. Instead, she frets about it, often allowing her emotions to impede her mastery of facts and procedures. I think Emily wants to know science, but she doesn't know it. How can that be? How can an obviously sharp young woman with good grades, apparent aptitude, and the requisite sense of responsibility fail to know science?

The answer lies in relation, in connection. As a youngster, Emily's relation with Anna and others enabled and encouraged her to construct relations and connections with natural phenomena, with her physical environment. Relation is a triadic reality; it does not consist, in everyday living, of face-to-face regard. It consists in interaction with a "third"—a phenomenon, an idea, an other. In any educative relation, the "teacher's" simultaneous interaction with the "subject matter" and the "student" opens spaces for the student's interaction with and connection to that subject matter. The generative relation to natural phenomena and scientific inquiry that Emily developed early in her life was not named "science." It had no name at all, but it existed. When formal instruction in the school subject of science began in the third grade, it prompted a slow but sure degeneration of Emily's knowledge of science as shared inquiry. She still "thinks like a scientist" to be sure, but that has no relation to science as she knows it. What she knows as science—the terminology, the facts, and the skills she repeats on tests—have no meaning for her. Worse, this knowledge pollutes her understanding of the world around her, prompting her to disdain any natural phenomena that are associated with her school study of science.

Emily's relationships with her teachers, especially her three designated science teachers since seventh grade, have been friendly. Their judgments of her have been positive. She doesn't hate her teachers. Why does she hate what they teach her? Because these teachers are ineffective in the only way that really matters from an educative point of view. They have not forged a relation with Emily that has scientific thought and understanding as its "third." Instead, they have treated her in a friendly but distant manner and offered her— utterly disconnected from any relation—knowledge of the earth, the oceans, the atmosphere, animals, plants, taxonomies, and elements, reactions in bite-size packages to be chewed and digested. She will have none of it. She just spits it back.

As a youngster, Emily was able to respond in relation to others and to natural phenomena in ways that could legitimately be labeled "scientific." That mode of responsiveness is now muted and moved to the background. It has been replaced in her educational foreground by a response-ability that is formulaic at best, by taxonomies and the periodic table. It is good that she is familiar with these staples of scientific theory and language, but this is a limited response to the possibilities of experience and meaning that science offers. I contend that Emily's response, this knowledge, is a predictable function of educational relations that do not enable her to know science as a collaborative inquiry.

Reading in relation

This relational account of science inquiry has its parallels in the story of Emily's reading habits. Emily was ready to read when she entered first grade. She set out quickly and settled into a pattern of above-grade-level reading competence. Good grades and standardized test scores confirmed our perception that she could read well. But she didn't. Read, I mean. She never read anything unless she absolutely had to. Textbook reading never really involved reading because she became adept at scanning the material, a skill for sure, but not a skill I would call "reading for understanding."

Emily very much liked being read to, as she had been as a young child by both Anna and by her extended family. She understood what was read to her and seemed to appreciate the interaction between herself and her reader. But this never prompted her to pick up the book that was being read on her own, or to seek out a similar book for purposeful or purely pleasure reading. In some ways, this was odd, incongruent with who Emily was and what was modeled for her. Both her father and I are readers, reading regularly for work, for enlightenment, and for entertainment. Her grandparents were also readers. She was regularly given books as gifts by thoughtful friends and family members who deliberately chose books that might appeal to her interests and abilities. And though Emily is a social creature, she is one who comfortably spends time alone entertaining herself. She virtually never used that time to read, however.

Occasionally, she was assigned a book to read for a school requirement. I don't remember whether she actually read those books or not. What I do remember is her unwillingness to read, her complaints and questions. "This book is stupid; why do I have to read this?" This pattern persisted until quite recently. The only book I ever heard her ask for was the second volume of *Chicken Soup for the Teenage Soul,* after the first had been given to her by her father as a birthday present.

Two years ago, everything changed. Emily was assigned to read any book from a school list that included several titles by Barbara Kingsolver. I had just finished reading Kingsolver's *Poisonwood Bible,* a work I found difficult to get into but incredibly provocative, rich, and rewarding. I suggested to Emily that she read it. She agreed, largely to meet a school requirement.

She started out and stalled, so I decided to read to her. Each evening, as my fourteen-year-old settled into bed, I sat beside her and read perhaps ten pages of Kingsolver's prose. Sometimes she nodded off as I read and we would back-track a page or two the following evening. Sometimes during the day, we would talk about what I had read the night before, about the cast of characters, their relationships and their locations in place and history. After about fifty pages, Emily simply picked up the book and kept reading. She finished *The Poisonwood Bible* in about two weeks, reading in odd moments as well as at bedtime, well before her school-imposed deadline. Most days I asked her what was happening now, who was where, what was being done. She would answer and we would exchange offhand comments about motivation or misunderstandings or mean-ings or future plot prospects. None of this was planned or formal; all of it was a function of our relationship on a day-to-day basis.

I am not exaggerating when I say that Emily has been reading, steadily and sometimes voraciously, ever since. Every night she reads before she falls asleep. She doesn't read as I do, several pages before turning out the light. She reads for a half hour or more, until I often have to tell her to turn out the light, wor-ried about the busy adolescent who is juggling a tough academic schedule and an even tougher athletic schedule.

What triggered Emily's transition from nonreader to reader? It wasn't only Barbara Kingsolver, though luck and timing may have made that a good title to capture Emily's interest. Perhaps it was the bribe (!) I offered Emily shortly af-ter the *Poisonwood Bible* episode. Summer was approaching and I told her that I would buy her one article of clothing for every book she read that summer after ninth grade. She started off fast, and a week into the summer we were heading off for the mall. Within two weeks, another book was completed and another article of clothing purchased. But then her motivation clearly shifted. Emily read as many as eight more books that summer, and I was not asked to "pay up" with any more clothing. The only time she struggled was when she was re-quired to read Cormac McCarthy's *All the Pretty Horses*. She resisted the assign-ment anyway and had no interest in or resonance with McCarthy's modern, but very male, coming-of-age story.

I believe the shift came when Emily began to think of reading as a function of her relation with me. I began to suggest books for her to read; she began to suggest books she read to me. Most of the books we have shared are not clas-sics: mysteries, Oprah Book Club selections, romantic novels, the Harry Potter series. Recently, she was required to select a biography to read for her American history class. I mentioned that I wanted to know more about Abigail Adams. Emily obtained a biography of Adams, read it for school, and passed it on to me.

Similarly, she has begun to trade books with friends. What one friend has read always becomes a topic of conversation with at least some of her other friends. Recommended titles are lent and borrowed, making their way from one friend to the next. Comments and judgments are exchanged casually. There is nothing formal about this interaction. There are no deadlines, nothing "assigned."

Emily continues to resist assigned reading. And the same friends who will share books and discuss them informally want no part of the books that they are all reading because of a course requirement. They complain about the book and the requirement even when the reading is not difficult, even when they find it of value. A recent experience with Arthur Miller's *The Crucible* is a case in point. Emily described to me her fascination with several of the aspects of Miller's morality play even as she was expressing dismay about having to read it. It seems that "assigned reading," like the subject of science, is an object of disdain, not because of what it is but because it does not issue from a relation, from a connection with others, with world, with self.

Emily is now a reader to the extent that reading is prompted by shared interest; that is, to the extent that it is a "third," an object of mutual interest and concern, in some relationship. For her and me, for instance, comparing notes on books we have read marks a new phase as mother and daughter. We are developing mutual interests and differentiating individualized interests revealed in reading an array of books. This does not simply mean that Emily reads only what others tell her to or what others also have an interest in. As I noted, she resists reading what her teacher tells her to read. She selects her own reading material, which she later recommends to others even as she accepts their recommendations. Nor does it mean that she only reads in the company of others; the actual act of reading is nearly always solitary. The point is that Emily has become (and continues to develop as) a reader as a by-product of her relation with others, friends and family. Her teachers for nine years were unable to bring this about despite, or maybe because of, regular required reading assignments. Such assignments were not about sharing reading as a function of a relationship, and they failed to accomplish their desired result for precisely that reason.

Double Movements

The stories told here are not only about Emily of course; they are also about me as parent, as educator, and as narrator/theorist. I encouraged the administration of Emily's IQ test. I offered both project ideas and procedural suggestions when she worked on science fair projects. I suggested Barbara Kingsolver, read to her, and reinforced her reading with new clothes. And I implicitly gave her permission to challenge right answers, to "hate science," and to refuse to read. I did so by giving her explicit permission to question the authority of tests and teachers. My actions were responses to Emily as I know her. One might object that I have shaped the events and colored the telling of the stories in making my point.

One might also object that these stories are quite particular. They describe specific educational circumstances in the life of a particular young woman who is white, relatively well-off, and supported psychologically and emotionally by parents and others. She lives in a particular region and neighborhood; she is physically and mentally healthy. Emily is not every young woman; she is one particular young woman. One might object that what is true of Emily is not true of the educational reality of all young persons.

While these objections are worth articulating, they are not central to the heart of the matter here. The validity and impact of these stories is independent of Emily's life circumstances or even of the accuracy with which I have portrayed her and her interactions. If these stories prompt others to review their own experience of knowing and coming to know through the lens of relation, they will have told their truth, whatever errors or shadings or standpoints they may express. My thesis will stand or fall on the extent to which others find their own knowing to be a function of relation. That has been my intention: to bring the reader to a recognition that relations with those who function in our lives as teachers determine the form *and* substance of our knowing, the knowing that shapes our responses to the people and circumstances of our lives. Hierarchical relations marked by obedience will generate the recitation of "right answers." Instrumental relations of input and output will allow no more than the representation of the results of *others'* scientific inquiry. Assigning readings instead of sharing common texts will result in a divorce of reading competence from reading for purpose or pleasure.

If, as educators, we want our students to develop lively, questioning, and not-always-conventional minds, we must engage them in relations with us that are marked by these qualities. If we want them to know and appreciate science as a shared mode of inquiry about the natural world, we must inquire with them. If we want them to read, they must come to know reading as an activity that challenges and changes minds; they must come to reading as the basis for communication with us.

Yet I fear that even the above formulation, attractive though it may seem, falls prey to the instrumental tendency that I highlighted earlier. When we begin educational efforts by specifying the "knowledge" or "knowing" that is the desired outcome, we unwittingly set limits on the educational experience of our students. We do not trust that our own wondering and inquiring and communicating with students will result in their knowing, in their developing ability to respond richly in relation to others and the world. Rich response requires the representation of funded knowledge, to be sure, but it also requires the ability to set funded knowledge aside in the pursuit of new understandings and new perspectives.

This is just one of the "double movements" that I find inherent in the three stories above and in activity that is genuinely educative. Knowledge of any kind or quality enables one to act but also limits potential response; it opens up vistas even as it sets up horizons. The point is not that Emily's original answer to the car/bike comparison question is better than her later answer. It is that her later answer extinguished the earlier one. She said it best: "Oh, I was so dumb then." Emily was not "dumb" in either instance. Her later answer was born of control, naming and managing the world for her ends. Her earlier answer was born of acceptance, of letting go, of taking the world as it presented itself to her. Education is about both, and educators themselves face the challenge of controlling and letting go even as they imagine the kind of interactions that will enable their students to master this double movement. Faith and trust are demanded as surely as intention and effort.

A second and related double movement requires that educators acknowledge responsibility for their actions even as they recognize that they are responding to circumstances that are not of their own making. Responsibility implies control; response suggests a lack of control. Educators are not responsible because they have control of the circumstances or persons to which they respond; rather, they are responsible because their actions, their responses, construct and reveal them(selves) as persons in the world. We recognize that we *can* and must respond, but we realize and accept that we can *only* respond.

We need to realize as well that our students can only respond. They encounter a world that is not at all under their control. They meet that world mediated through those who function as educators. Anna took the world as it came; Emily learned to do the same. Science teachers imposed control on what mattered; Emily responded with resistance. I opened the door to the world of books that is my leisure; Emily entered. In each case, Emily came to know her educator and, in knowing the educator, developed knowledge congruent with the mediating relation. She is responsible because her answers reveal her coming to be; but she can only respond. Her response is a function of her being in relation.

I am not arguing that relations in education are more important than knowledge and knowing. I am suggesting that they are rooted one in the other, that the very idea of knowledge depends on the presence of relation and vice versa. Every experience that purports to be educational has some notion of knowledge and some quality of relation intertwined at its core. Unfortunately, concepts of knowledge and knowing are linked in contemporary imagination to accountability and control, but not to response-ability and acceptance. That

view of knowledge dominates the professional education landscape, leaving little room to perceive, let alone consider, the human relations that motivate
learning and growing. These relations ought to be primary from an educator's
standpoint; the double movement of constructing and accepting certain qualities of relation between teacher and student is what makes possible (though
never totally determinable) desirable qualities of knowing.

Educators' (and parents') goals for students ultimately reside not in academic standards and instructional objectives but in who we are as persons. We
want our students to be, loosely speaking, who we are in our best moments. But
we also want them to be better than we are. We want them to know what we
know and to respond to others and the world in the ways that we can and do,
and we want them to stretch beyond our capability to respond. This will not
happen until they come to know us and we come to know them. We meet to
learn. Our meeting, our relation, matters. It determines the form and structure
of our knowledge, the knowing that issues in action. Knowing is response-able
relation.

READING RELATIONS

Rosalie M. Romano

Meno: But how will you look for something when you don't in the least know what it is? How on earth are you going to set up something you don't know as the object of your search? To put it another way, even if you come right up against it, how will you know that what you have found is the thing you didn't know?[1]

The notion of relation in education has come to refer to a wide range of educational philosophies and curriculum interactions. Even in the perspectives offered in this book on pedagogy of relations, that pedagogy does not stand for any unitary approach. However, it does refer to a coalition of educational interests committed to engaging with modes of social change and educational reform for teachers and students. While the authors in this volume share a number of assumptions, assumptions such as the primacy of social relations in education, how we all look at pedagogies of relations cannot be harnessed in a particular philosophy or approach. The perspective I offer is based on my search for openings and spaces to help new teachers develop a deep awareness of the primacy of relations.

My search for openings with these teachers involves questions such as these: Who are the students they will teach? How will they come to know them? How will they learn to teach in such a way that students want to engage in learning? While these seem orthodox questions in teacher preparation, the approaches used in much coursework, and in many university programs, may miss the mark in fostering a disposition that is sensitive to "reading" students so that a teacher might better reach them. Frequently, college professors may not go into K-12 schools to keep abreast of the complexities and pressures that classroom teachers face. Yet those professors likely send their preservice teachers into K-12 schools for field experiences, so students can become familiar with the cadence of the classroom through observation and guided teaching. Where and how will new teachers be introduced and cultivated into the awareness of a pedagogy of relations? The pedagogy of which I write is a different type of literacy, a literacy that _reads_ students so that teachers might keep in touch with who their students are, so they might be responsive, and be conscious of those teachable moments that can unpredictably appear as quickly as they can disappear if a teacher remains unaware of them.

This chapter will discuss the facets that influence the development of a literacy of relations so that new teachers can "read" relations with their students. I begin with the difficult work classroom teachers must face each day, and I ask the reader to think of the preservice teacher placed in a classroom, a teacher who is idealistic and naïve, or at least unaware of the contradictions and ironies that abound in schools. From classrooms, I move to critical literacy in reading, and I focus on the different forms or levels of reading that pass for literacy education. Then I will examine the reflections of a group of middle childhood student teachers the year before they move into their student teaching experience, student teachers who engage in an Interactive Performance about social issues for high school students. I use Interactive Performance to raise the awareness and consciousness of student teachers to foster insight about how students think about these issues.

Classrooms Where New Teachers Are Placed

Modeling for new teachers is complicated by the conditions under which the majority of cooperating teachers must work. These school conditions set up divisions and barriers, invisible but nevertheless palpable and effective, enculturating teachers into becoming separated from their students. Classroom teachers, particularly in this period of test frenzy, are beset from all sides with constituents telling them what to do. Administrators exhort teachers to "raise those test scores" at all costs. Districts spend funds earmarked for curriculum on mandated practice test booklets required to be used in all classrooms by teachers in districts that are on "academic watch." Parents, who themselves may remember their schooling as primarily drill-and-kill approaches to stuffing facts into their heads, equate test scores with "learning." The manifestation of behaviorist and instrumental emphasis on measurement and outcomes focuses the educational vision narrowly, and also focuses intensely on passing test scores, thus reducing or rendering invisible the thousands of moments in each teacher's day when a word, a look, a gesture of encouragement, or a nod of acceptance moves a student toward growth. The increasingly mechanistic approach to teaching, based on behaviorist approaches, renders the essential oil of teaching into sound bites of direct instruction, phonemes, and words disconnected from context. Students are expected to stand at the conveyor belt of "wisdom," picking pieces of information up as fast as they can.

Such a daily grind of learning is not only a labor for teachers and students, but frequently results in a crowding out of the richness and satisfaction of being in a classroom: crowded out is a sense of belonging, a sense of care. This chapter focuses on teacher preparation, a preparation of new teachers through a program that deliberately seeks to forge educative communities.[2]

> Meno: But how will you look for something when you don't in the least know what it is? How on earth are you going to set up something you don't know as the object of your search? To put it another way, even if you come right up against it, how will you know that what you have found is the thing you didn't know?

What is this "something" to which Meno alludes? If we look at colleges of education, this "something" is interpreted by many in teacher preparation programs as the "science of teaching." Men and women enter a teacher preparation program filled with idealism, hope, and a desire to connect students with new understanding. These same men and women exit their teacher preparation program assured that they know the object of their search: how to teach their students. That teacher education programs may be missing the "object" of the search is revealed in the high percentage of new teachers who do not or cannot continue to teach in our nation's schools beyond five years. "Something" is missing when idealistic, hopeful teachers, who know they are not entering a profession that will compensate through either salary or recognition, within five years leave the classroom with neither idealism nor hope intact. External instead of internal expectations become the beacon for new teachers, looking to a principal and textbooks to dictate how and what to teach.

In this climate of utilitarianism in teacher preparation, there is neither room nor attention in the curriculum to learn to foster an educative community in the classroom. Preservice teachers are given a diet of cognitive development, methods, technology, and perhaps one philosophical foundations course as part of their teacher preparation program. Along with these courses are added the reading courses to promote the teaching of literacy to students. For example, in Ohio, a minimum of three courses on reading development, reading diagnosis, and reading in the content area are required for teacher licensure. Where are the courses dedicated to the conditions for cultivating a classroom where wonder, complexity, and discovery are privileged in teacher preparation? Meno's question comes back to the forefront: How will you look for something when you don't in the least know what it is? That "something" is the quality of relations that, ideally, exists and is constituted in a classroom, and throughout the entire school.

What is too often overlooked in teacher preparation is the quality of relations with students that is necessary for fostering engaged learning and thinking, and that fosters a social construction of knowledge. Instead, teacher preparation focuses on *how* to teach rather than on the dispositions required to foster engaged learning in students. This learning will always be social in some aspect, for knowledge construction does not occur in some vacuum, but in an evolving knowledge *culture* as students make sense of complexity and ambiguity.

Toward a Powerful Literacy of Relations

A framework for thinking about preparing teachers for such a disposition toward relations exists in the literature on literacy. In fact, the idea for developing literacy for relations began in the discussion and debate over what literacy is. For our purposes here, literacy is defined as a complex and interactive process of interpretation that occurs within a social and cultural context where students live and learn in relation to one another. These relations are built on trust and caring about one another's well-being. Further, a fundamental form of learning is predicated on a student being part of a community of learners that values the search for understanding. The word "literacy" is used liberally throughout all sectors of education as well as in society to mean the same thing: to read. However, being able "to read" holds different meanings to those who understand the power of the written and spoken word. There are levels of literacy that impact and have implications for students and teachers, often hidden from the teachers themselves as they proceed to teach their students "to read." Patrick Finn analyzes literacy and links different levels to socioeconomic levels of both students and teachers. It is important for this chapter to attend to Finn's argument about these different levels before we apply the notion of literacies of reading to the notion of literacies of relations between students and teachers.

Finn argues for teachers to promote and teach their students, in particular those who are disenfranchised, a "literacy with an attitude." By this, he exhorts teachers to move beyond low levels of literacy that can be found at many poor and working-class classrooms today. Building on the work of Jean Anyon, Finn identifies four different levels of literacy that are taught uncritically by teachers depending on the social class of their students. The first level is performative. At the performative level, students can sound out words and write conversational sentences. This is a concretized form of reading, with little thought given to meaning making. Spelling and phonetics are primarily valued, and the value of contextual understanding or motivation is either diminished or not acknowledged at all.

The second level of literacy Finn describes is functional literacy. Functional literacy emphasizes following directions, reading directions, understanding directions. These two levels of literacy, performative and functional, are prevalent in poor and working-class schools where students come from backgrounds that are urban or rural poor. Building on Anyon's research, Finn argues that these two levels of literacy are meant to produce students who can follow directions when told what to do in order to reproduce social and economic structures.

Performative and functional literacies become the aim of teachers in poor, working-class schools. Students are not expected to question, challenge, or intellectually engage with learning. Instead, the "good" teacher is one whose classrooms are quiet and orderly, where students do their work obediently.

Schools that serve higher socioeconomic middle-class students focus on the third level of informational literacy. Teachers who teach informational literacy expect performative and functional literacies in their students as well as informational, which teaches about how to read for information, how to write reports based on this information, and how to take examinations. In informational literacy, students are expected to comply with directions, but there is more independence in the work that teachers demand of students. Projects and term papers are part of the assignments for students to demonstrate that they can read for information and can tell what they read.

It is, however, what Finn calls powerful literacy that exists in abundance in schools that serve the upper-middle and the upper classes. In such schools, powerful literacy is taught to students, assuming the first three levels of performative, functional, and informational. This powerful literacy requires "creativity and reason—the ability to evaluate, analyze and synthesize what is read."[3] One way of looking at powerful literacy is that it demands of those who are learning it to live it together in the classroom because it is a literacy that must be interpreted socially within some context in order to be interpreted and understood. As such, it is a dynamic literacy that shifts according to perspectives read and perspectives shared in order to construct both understanding and knowledge. It is an active literacy, this powerful literacy, asking students to participate, engage, interpret, analyze, and rethink.

Applying these important characteristics of the four levels of literacy to human relations, particularly in the classroom, I will argue that it is powerful literacy that teacher preparation programs should explicitly teach preservice teachers to develop in order to read their students through "creativity and reason—the ability to evaluate, analyze and synthesize." Developing a powerful literacy of relations is a challenge to teacher educators because the students they teach are more likely to bring with them educations that emphasized informational literacy, the third level Finn ascribes to schools of the middle class, to which a large majority of new teachers belong. Even if education professors acknowledge and teach about these different levels of literacy, students may still not realize a powerful literacy as the "object" of learning, as a powerful paradigm for how to reach their students. "How on earth are you going to set up something you don't know as the object of your search?"

Reading Relations

For preservice teachers to cultivate a powerful literacy of relations, then, is a challenge on many levels, especially if new teachers are themselves from working-class and middle-class backgrounds and have little or no experiences with powerful literacy in their own schooling. Like those students from poor, working-class backgrounds who are exposed only to functional and performative literacy, preservice teachers can be taught only through explicit interpretation on the part of teacher educators.

In my work with new teachers, I have collaborated with a performing artist on campus to work with my class of preservice teachers to develop a script and to perform a play that reflects social (and often social justice) issues that concern middle and high school students. I place my students in schools for the quarter, working with cooperative teachers to teach lessons, to learn to assess student learning, and do other teacherly activities. However, a crucial part of the field experience assignment is to have lunch with students, or to participate in after-school activities with them throughout the quarter. The purpose of this is to learn to listen to students and find out their worries or concerns.

A few weeks before the end of the quarter, I bring in the actor/director to team-teach the reflection seminar for these student teachers. At that time, we brainstorm the issues that seem to have emerged from listening and conversing with the middle and high school students. The actor/director guides the class into identifying those issues they believe are most pressing for students. When four or five of these issues are identified, the actor/director breaks the student teachers into cooperative groups. These groups meet together to develop characters and a plot that includes the issue or issues that they have chosen from the four or five. Developing the plot and character is demanding work and often involves a number of extra hours outside of class, working together with the actor/director. When the script is written, all groups meet together in a large group and rehearse their draft of their script. Other groups listen and critique whether characters are believable, whether the scenery is authentic, and then they make suggestions. When scripts are written and rehearsed, all of us go into a local school and present our Interactive Performance for each class in that school.

The Interactive Performance is the creation of the actor/director, who is completing a research project on this technique. What makes an Interactive Performance different than a regular play is that at the end of each of its two or three acts, the characters (the student teachers) come back on stage (usually the front of the classroom) and, with the actor/director as the facilitator, answer questions the students in the audience ask of their characters. The responses must be in the character (role) they are in, so leaps of imagination must accompany replies to the questions and comments the students in the audience raise about how their character acted or what their character said to other characters in the play. I try to schedule an Interactive Performance with each of my preservice teacher courses on foundations and pedagogy. For the majority of students who come to my class for the first time, Interactive Performance is bewildering and irrelevant to them, as indicated by a typical reflective comment by a student who, along with her peers, only later came to awareness, as a future teacher, of the significance of understanding students:

> So when we first started I was kind of confused as to the whole point of these performances. As we started making up the characters and the script I saw that they were really in-depth plays about everyday life, about issues that the students need to see and need to discuss that sometimes get swept under the carpet because people are too afraid to talk about them.

One play was developed around the tension of boyfriend/girlfriend relationships with one girl ("Susan") who was gay.[4] The high school audience asked pertinent questions of the characters in the play, but they were more interested in the heterosexual relationships. Only at the end of the play, after the second scene, did one high schooler broach the topic of why Susan wasn't talking about which boy she was with. Susan, in character, had to respond as to her reasons. This future middle childhood teacher wrote this in her reflective journal after the performance:

> Through the interactive performance I remembered what it felt like to be a student again. I played a homosexual girl who had not come out to anyone except one of her friends. It made me realize that if I am this uncomfortable telling a class (in my role) this information what it must be like for a student actually going through this.

Susan's response above was representative of the other student teachers, who found that by playing the role of a young adolescent grappling with an issue that was important to adolescents, there was a strong identification with the struggles students have with relationships. Susan was able to see herself from the view of other students, but she also made what I call a leap of imaginative compassion when she felt the confusion and angst as if she were the young girl herself. How does this carry over into becoming a teacher who can read students?

Middle and high school teachers see up to 160 students per day in their courses. The grind of teaching comes from constraints of curriculum and schedule, where you are to teach a subject for anywhere between thirty and eighty minutes to a classroom full of students. (When I taught in an inner-city school, it was not unusual for me to have thirty-five students in one fifty-minute class. With five classes a day, plus students assigned to me as advisees, I carried class loads of over 175 students a day for the entire school year.) A teacher can become numb or inured to the travails of students, especially since young adolescents tend to dramatize events or issues that positively or negatively affect them. Keeping aware, awake, and attentive to students requires a particular disposition for teachers, especially in such demanding environments. A teacher may or may not value or ever learn explicitly what it means and what it feels like to be aware of the cadence of students' responses to issues. Susan has had occasion through the Interactive Performance to experience for a moment the pain and confusion of a student's struggle. Will she be able to transfer this imaginative compassion to other situations with other students? This is my aim, of course. And I think that now she has a sense of what it is to experience life from the students' perspective, she will at least have been made aware of the primacy of relations in her life as a future teacher.

Another play dealt with the identified issue of socioeconomic class and the differential treatment students get from teachers, counselors, administrators, and other school personnel. Southeastern Ohio, where Ohio University is located, is in the foothills of Appalachia, where poor and working-class communities struggle with dwindling resources, the closing of coal and iron mines, and a culture of poverty. Students from poor, working-class homes attend school with peers who are much more privileged, peers who have one or both parents on university faculty or who work in another capacity within the university, peers who could be identified as middle- or upper-middle-class. In middle and high school, the division of the students falls between socioeconomic classes, even more than race or gender. Students who are from poor and working-class backgrounds are aware and often vocal about how they are treated by teachers and counselors. This Interactive Performance revolved around a counselor who voluntarily gave a middle-class student an application to a university after a working-class student had asked for a college application and was given a local community college application. This touched a sore point in the high school audience. The student teacher who played the counselor was moved by the experience to say:

> Even when the tension in the room began to rise I tried to stay in character. I could almost *feel* [emphasis mine] the angry stares they were giving me. I think the students saw they could do something about Mrs. Smiths [the counselor] in their lives. I am glad I played a character who is the complete opposite of myself. It made me think about how other people can think and how they can affect different students in different ways.

The student teacher who played "Jim" reflects:

I could *sense* [emphasis mine] the passion in some of the students as they became angry at some of the characters in the performance. I played the role of an average student with a desire to further my education that was almost sidetracked by a biased guidance counselor. I [felt that] the students were on my side and [that they] quickly discovered the disguised injustice [of the counselor].

In real life, Jim comes from an upper-middle-class background, and during the debriefing after the Interactive Performances he continued to churn over the vehemence of the students about class issues. He hadn't been aware of his own class before, even though he had courses in diversity in education and was committed to paying attention to trying to understand his students who come from poor, working-class, and other backgrounds different from his. The impact of the high school students' "passion" made a mark on him. He not only is aware of what was invisible before, but, because his role was as a student who was discriminated against, Jim desires to understand and learn how to relate in supportive ways to students of all classes.

In the same performance, the student playing the role of the privileged student ("Jane"), reflects about the same experience:

I really enjoyed performing. I never imagined that the character I played would be so intense. It was amazing to be able to learn about and become another person. Although I was pretty unsure that our skit would come together, I was amazed how we all worked together and how that students seemed to really grasp the message we were trying to get across.

She, too, was able to "read" students as a performer in the play. What makes Interactive Performance such an interesting and potentially powerful parallel to teaching is that the teachers can guide but cannot predict either the reaction or the questions that the students will ask. The discomfort level of the student teachers in their characters, regardless of their role, is centered on the unpredictability of the situation. They feel vulnerable in front of students, fearing they will not know what to say or do. This state of vulnerability, even though filtered through their roles in the play, offers a significant opening to foster a need to read the students in the audience. In short: Teachers need to learn the literacy of reading their students. At first this specific literacy of relations may be motivated by the situation of being a student teacher. However, an additional effect is deepened by taking the role of a student. This is the jolt of the imaginative compassion, feeling and seeing the world from a student's point of view. The privileged student writes:

Each time that I have done the Interactive Performance I have thoroughly enjoyed it and learned a lot from the issues we are trying to raise with our students. It's funny how addressing the issues through our performance not only raises my awareness of them, but also stimulates my thinking about how I would deal with the issues in my own classroom.

The last Interactive Performance I will share revolved around abusive behavior and racism. "Lisi" describes her perspective in her role:

> My character was Lisi, a 14-year-old ninth grader who kind of sticks up for the foreign exchange student who was abused by her boyfriend, especially when her friend Stephanie says that it's because she's from Peru, and "everyone from Peru is treated that way." Lisi is also against drinking because one of her brother's friends was in a really bad alcohol-related car accident and nearly died. I thought that it was really neat that all of the characters dealt with some kind of issue that could be discovered, challenged, and was a learning experience. I think that the students at the high school responded really well to the skits. They were all listening and very attentive, you could tell that you were getting through to them on a level that they could relate to, understand, and work with.

The student teacher who played the abusive boyfriend had this to say:

> I really enjoyed and learned from the feedback and reactions to our performance students gave us. Especially the girl who called me a jerk and took my character to task. It was very difficult to play a person I would never be like in real life. As the students asked me to account for my behavior, I came to see how articulate and serious they are about their friendships. This is something I will remember as a future eighth and ninth grade teacher!!

Conclusion

> Meno asks: But how will you look for something when you don't in the least know what it is? How on earth are you going to set up something you don't know as the object of your search? To put it another way, even if you come right up against it, how will you know that what you have found is the thing you didn't know?

My object was to set up conditions under which preservice teachers needed to pay attention to the behaviors and responses of students in order to be able to explicitly discuss and guide them into learning how to interpret the cues and clues all students give to their teachers about what they are thinking and feeling. This is the primary condition for literacy of relations: Teachers have to be aware of the object of their search before they can see it. In the case of teachers, relations are invisible to the majority of new teachers, who are beset with experiences, assumptions, and coursework in their program that turn their attention outward instead of inward. Parker Palmer claims that we teacher educators prepare new teachers to be autonomous and independent of the students they teach.[5] Without our conscious understanding that we cannot be teachers without our students, teachers new and old perpetuate school as the conveyor-belt system it is for far too many students today who feel disenfranchised, disconnected, and dismissed by education and educators. School becomes dead space for students, without mission, focus, or participation, without a set of issues that have anything to do with their lives.

Like powerful critical literacy, reading relations between students and teachers finds its partner in a social arena, often in studying social justice issues. Becoming literate in relations is a journey for teachers because it is dynamic and dependent on inner capacity, resources, and a disposition to understand and be responsive to students. This cannot be told or directed or demanded of teachers. Instead, it must be cultivated under the conditions that foster teachers wanting to know. This need to know was present and strong during and after the Interactive Performances, and it provided the avenue for a dialogue and reflection that moved us as a class, teacher educator and student teachers, onto a new plane of understanding and perspectives of the primacy of relations. While we may not have reached the object of our search, we did become aware that a search was needed. At this point, their journey as teachers had begun.

Notes

1. Plato, *The Meno*, trans. W. K. C. Guthrie, in E. Hamilton and H. Cairns eds., *The Collected Dialogues of Plato* (Princeton, NJ: Princeton University Press), 363.
2. Rosalie Romano, *Forging an Educative Community: The Wisdom of Love, the Power of Understanding, and the Terror of It All* (New York: Peter Lang Publishing, 2000).
3. Finn, Patrick, *Literacy with an Attitude: Educating Working-Class Students in Their Own Self-Interest* (Albany, NY: SUNY Press, 1999), 121–127.
4. No names are real, either of the student teachers or their characters.
5. Parker Palmer, *The Courage to Teach: Exploring the Inner Landscape of a Teacher's Life* (San Francisco: Jossey Bass, 1998).

PERSONAL AND SOCIAL RELATIONS IN EDUCATION

Barbara J. Thayer-Bacon

The term *relation* is ambiguous. Relation signifies the existential connections, a dynamic and functional interaction; it also signifies the logical relationships of terms. We speak of the overlapping and interconnecting of concepts and meanings, and we describe how things affect each other ontologically. Relationships can be personal, one-on-one exchanges as between a teacher and a student, a parent and a child, or between two lovers. We also use the term *relational* in a general manner, to describe social relationships between citizens and their country, or the relationship of men and women. We speak of relations in terms of kinship, and we say we can relate to someone else, meaning we feel sympathy toward that person or we can compare our experiences to the other. The plural use of the term *relations* is even used to mean sexual intercourse. Given all the different ways we use this term, *relations* has a common theme of "connection" to others, which is what I want it to signify. I find it an advantage, not a disadvantage, that relation means connections in so many ways. My hope is that its many uses will remind us of the transactional nature of knowing (in the Deweyan sense of the term).[1]

For my contribution to this book, I would like to explore some of the important implications of a relational approach to knowing for education in terms of personal and social relations. The definition of education is much debated, and we can find a contribution to that debate in the work of Gert Biesta within this volume. For my purposes here, I will assume that education is a studenting-teaching process that involves a teacher and a student (whose roles are fluid, flexible, and often interchangeable) and something that is taught (the curriculum, the content) in some kind of setting and in some manner (the form of instruction, the context). I will look at how the roles of teachers and students change within a school setting, given a relational focus, and I want to consider curriculum issues. We will find that a relational theory of knowing has tremendous implications for all areas of schooling as we know them today in much of the world.

This discussion concerning personal and social relations fits within a larger project of mine, the development of what I call a relational (e)pistemology.[2] A relational (e)pistemology is an approach to knowing that emphasizes that knowledge is something that is socially constructed by embedded and embodied people who are in relations with each other and their greater environment. We are fallible, our criteria are corrigible, and our standards are socially constructed, and thus continually in need of critique and reconstruction. A relational approach argues that knowing is something people develop as they have experiences with each other and the world around them. People improve on ideas that have been socially constructed and passed down to them by others. They do this improving by further developing their understandings and enlarging their connections. With enlarged relationships, people are able to create new meanings for their experiences. An (e)pistemology that rests on an assumption of fallibility entails pluralism, both in terms of there being no one final Answer at the end of inquiring, and also in terms of the need to be open and inclusive of others who help us compensate for our own limitations. A relational (e)pistemology strives for awareness of context and values, and seeks to tolerate vagueness and ambiguities.

I will rely on assorted examples available: my own and others' experiences as teachers and students; the various conversations I have shared with others concerning schools; and the tools of intuition, emotions, imagination, and reason I/we have available to help me/us constructively think of some new possibilities for schools.[3] I will try to remind the reader of my own limitations and fallibility throughout the discussion by revealing my own biases and not neglecting my own contextuality. I do not want to try to ignore and diminish the political power that philosophers wield in their social roles as legitimators. I do not mean to suggest that the examples I offer or the suggestions I make are in any way final or complete, for I have argued elsewhere for the impossibility of attaining knowledge that is certain, as well as for the impossibility of attaining knowledge that is universal.[4] As a fallible social critic, I need others to contribute to this discussion and help me in this redescribing effort. I need a clamor of diverse voices, so I encourage your contributions to help us in our efforts to recreate anew schools that take relations to be primary.

Personal Relations

As we learn in Bonnie Lyon McDaniel's and Cherlyn Pijanowski's papers within this volume, psychoanalytic philosophers focus on intimate relationships we share, as infants, with our childcare providers. More spiritually focused philosophers, such as Martin Buber and Simone Weil, focus on a very intimate relationship that we share as spiritual beings with our Thou.[5] By "intimate" I do not mean sexual, I mean relationships that are close associations, relationships between I and Thou, between one-caring and one-cared-for. Feminist scholars such as Jane Flax, Sarah Ruddick, and Nel Noddings emphasize that all of us begin our lives already in relation with our biological mothers, and that this very close relationship extends for us into the early years of our lives, according to object relations theory, as we continue the psychological birthing process with our adoptive mothers.[6] It is through our personal relationships with others that we develop a voice, an "I," a sense of who we are as unique individuals in relation to Thou. In her book *Caring*, Nel Noddings does not just explore the intimate relationship of a mother and child in her discussion of caring relations, but she also considers the relationship between a teacher and student as another example of a caring relationship. She further explores the personal relationship between teachers and students in her follow-up book, *The Challenge to Care in Schools*.[7]

Noddings's description of teacher-student relationships in terms of one-caring and one-cared-for is considered controversial in the United States for many reasons, one of which is the distinction that Americans make between private and public relations. It is expected that parents and their children, and friends and lovers, have close personal relationships; these are all considered examples of private relationships. Teachers and students, and bosses and their employees, are expected to have a public relationship that is therefore not intimate and personal. In the United States, we fear that if teachers establish personal relationships with their students this means that students will be vulnerable to manipulation and indoctrination, including physical and psychological abuse. We recognize that teachers wield great power over students in their roles as dispensers of knowledge and evaluators and judges of what students have learned. Teachers assign grades to students' work, and these grades help to determine whether or not students have the opportunity for the good life, in terms of employment and higher education. We also recognize that teachers are responsible for the safety and well-being of their students, and we realize that teachers have great influence on the quality of students' daily lives as a result of teacher interactions with others. Teachers witness and monitor students' behavior.

Yet certainly parents (childcare providers) wield even greater power over their children than schoolteachers. In fact, children's very survival depends on their parents, and still we acknowledge the importance of parents establishing personal relationships with their children. We even argue that if parents are unable or unwilling to establish caring relationships with their children, those children could be hindered in their growth and development and will have to find ways to compensate for this lack. If caring is so important in parental relationships despite even greater risk of abuse, why is the establishment of caring relationships with students not important for teachers in school settings? I want to suggest that in fact it is very important for teachers to establish caring relationships with their students. One of the most vital implications of taking relations as primary is that those of us working in schools need to focus our attention on the relationships teachers have with their students, as well as the relationships students have with each other. A relational approach to knowing describes knowers as social beings-in-relation-with-others, not as isolated individuals. As social beings-in-relation-with-others, we must not only focus on relationships, but also ensure that these relationships are caring rather than harmful, oppressive ones. Focus on relational education recognizes and attempts to address the political powers involved in relationships, both personally and socially.

Schools in America currently focus predominantly on the outcomes and products of schooling. Often these are entirely disconnected from the relational processes of learning. Students become objects who must produce a certain amount and quality of products in order to graduate, and teachers become the managers of this production effort, whose job security and salaries depend on how productive their students are. Current emphasis on proficiency exams in the United States, attempts to hold teachers accountable and make sure all students are able to produce the predetermined outcomes, only further enhance a product focus. A relational approach to education insists that we must focus on the process of learning and consider very deeply how we can help students, as social beings-in-relation-with-others, become knowers. While all are born with the possibility of becoming knowers, we can only actualize that possibility if others, such as our family members and friends and schoolteachers, encourage and support our efforts.

I am suggesting that schooling (and the larger process of educating) at its best is a personal, relational process between a student and a teacher. I want to suggest, in agreement with Noddings, that teachers need to establish caring relationships with their students, in which students are active participants able to reject relationships with their teachers if the latter are not perceived as caring. While there are many false forms of caring, a genuine caring relationship is one that is good, not harmful to either the one-caring or the one-cared-for.[8] A caring relationship is based on treating the other with respect and dignity, so that a trusting relationship can develop between the two. In a caring relationship, teachers must focus their efforts on valuing and appreciating students' needs and learning what their interests and desires are. Teachers should, as far as possible, suspend their own beliefs, feelings, and values and listen attentively and generously to their students. This is the only way they can be assured of coming close to understanding their students, and can therefore help to meet students' needs to know. This effort of attending to the needs of others helps assure us that the teaching-student relationship will be a caring one, and not one that is manipulative or harmful to the student or teacher.

In most middle schools, high schools, and colleges in America, it is next to impossible for teachers to establish caring relationships with their students. The larger the population in the school is and the more students each individual teacher has, the more difficult the establishing of caring teacher-student relationships becomes. It is not humanly possible to establish caring relationships with a large number of people. There is just not enough time in each day to be able to listen attentively to everyone. One teacher can only be available, approachable, and attentive to so many people, and most teachers are asked to teach more students than they can possibly get to know well. Not only are teachers and students not able to establish caring relationships with each other in most upper-level schools, but also students are not able to establish caring relationships with other students either, for there are too many students in each classroom and too little time to get to know each other.

Even though we make it difficult for teachers to establish caring relationships with their students due to the working conditions, it is easy to point to examples that show we do value caring teacher-student relationships. Schools, including colleges, will advertise that one of their advantages is their smaller number of students, and they will boast about their student-teacher ratio as a way to attract students to their school. They will point out that the smaller the student-teacher ratio, the more likely that individual students will receive the attention they need from their teachers to help them learn. Schools that offer flexible, alternative forms of scheduling where students can enjoy more time with their teachers and the possibility of having their teachers as mentors throughout their schooling experience will advertise these possibilities as ways to attract students to their campus. Again, the schools will acknowledge the value of students being able to work closely and over extended periods of time with their teachers, for it helps the students learn and succeed in school. And campuses will offer faculty smaller numbers of classes to teach and fewer students as incentives to teach there. They will point out that faculty teaching there have more time to prepare for their classes as well as more time with their students. The gift of more time and fewer students will make it more likely that potential faculty members will be able to do a good job as teachers and enjoy the intrinsic rewards of teaching, such as getting to know their students and watching them grow as a result of working with them. In general, the more prestigious the university, college, elementary, or secondary school is, the smaller the faculty-student ratio is and the lighter the faculty teaching load is.

The closest the majority of students in public schools come to being able to establish caring relationships with their teachers and their classmates is when students are in preschool, kindergarten, and lower elementary grades. Several states in the United States have established public policies limiting the number of students who can be in lower grade levels to no more than twenty, and often each classroom will have two teachers or a teacher and a classroom aide (non-certified teacher). Again, such policies demonstrate that we do recognize the value of teacher-student relationships. With no more than twenty students, two adults, and most of each day to be together, there is much more of a chance for students and teachers to establish caring relationships with each other.

Sometimes students will have the opportunity to establish caring relationships with teachers if they are placed in special education or bilingual education classes, for these teachers may teach the same students for up to three years, depending on their school's resources and policies. Also, some smaller public schools only have one art, music, foreign language, or physical education teacher, and so that teacher will have the same students for extended periods of time, sometimes stretching over the entire time the student is enrolled in the school. However, many of these teachers are severely limited in terms of the amount of time they spend with students and are even more overwhelmed by the sheer number of students enrolled in a school if they are the only gym, art, or music teacher for the entire school enrollment. Even worse, they can be the "specials" teacher for two or three schools.

As a Montessori teacher, I had even more opportunity to establish caring relationships with my students than most elementary teachers.[9] Not only were my classroom sizes smaller (the largest class I had was twenty-three students), I also had classroom co-teachers, and the students were in my classroom for most of the day. I also had the students in my classroom for three years. Three years of time with a student makes a big difference, and that is the typical structure for Montessori classrooms; students ages 3–6, 6–9, and 9–12 years are together in the same room for three years. As some students graduate each year and move on, and other, younger students move into the classroom each year, the child ideally stays in the same room, with the same teacher, and a core of other students around the same age, for three years. I found that as a teacher in such a setting not only was it possible for me to establish caring relationships with my students, it was necessary. Neither the students nor I could look forward to another year of being together unless we were able to relate to each other in a caring manner. And students could not function effectively with the same students in their classroom year after year unless they were able to learn how to get along. My classroom became like an extended family, which included the students' family members as well, many of whom I still hear from.

I am not suggesting that teachers and students need to establish caring relationships in schools because students are lacking these experiences in their home settings, as Jane Roland Martin does in her book *The Schoolhome,* though that is sadly often true.[10] Like Noddings, I want to suggest that even students experiencing significant caring relationships in their home settings will benefit from experiencing caring relationships with their teachers. The establishment of personal, close relationships with teachers and peers will help students become knowers able to participate in and contribute to the knowing process. It will help them develop their own voice and learn how to express it, for they can feel confident that others will listen generously. And they will be able to learn from other students' voices as well. It will help them gain confidence in their own abilities, for they will feel valued and affirmed by the attention they receive. Students will thrive under such conditions. Why should only a few students be allowed the opportunity to experience close, personal relationships with their teachers and other students—those who come from wealthy families, attend Montessori schools, or live in small, isolated locations? There are many things we can do to help make it possible for all students and teachers to experience caring relationships.

One suggestion is to make classroom sizes smaller, following the early childhood/younger elementary policy of no more than twenty students in a classroom. Another suggestion is to assign more than one teacher to a classroom. A third suggestion is to lengthen the time students spend in one classroom with each other and their teachers, as well as increase the number of times students can have the same teacher. Some schools are trying similar ideas, such as changing their scheduling formats to what many are calling "block scheduling," which gives students more time in a classroom each day with a teacher. Other schools are creating "schools within schools" as ways of breaking down large student populations into smaller groups, and having the same teachers work as a team with the same students, so students can become better known in a more holistic manner by their teachers and classmates. Some schools are creating advising/mentoring programs where all teachers are assigned a small number of students to meet with regularly and consistently throughout the student's enrollment in school. These and other related practices will help students and teachers have more chances to develop personal relationships with each other.

Now, let's come back to the concerns people express about the studenting-teaching relationship being a personal, caring one. In no way am I suggesting that any student, or teacher for that matter, should have to experience a teaching-studenting relationship with someone who is manipulative or abusive. Students should not have to fear their teachers or protect themselves from teachers (or vice versa). Many teachers do not know how to relate to other people in healthy, constructive ways, and they use teaching as an opportunity to dominate and oppress others. These people should not be allowed to harm our children. And unfortunately, today there are many students who are so troubled that they are a danger to other students and teachers as well. These students should not be allowed to harm each other or their teachers. But these are extreme examples that are signs of unhealthy social conditions. The extremes do not diminish the importance of establishing caring relationships with each other; they underscore how important caring relationships are. A relational approach to education, and (e)pistemology, describes knowers as social beings-in-relation-with-others, not as isolated individuals. It therefore emphasizes that education is a relational process between beings who are in relation with each other. Wherever people are together in relation with each other there will be political factors. A relational approach to knowing does not seek the impossible task of getting rid of political factors, nor does it try to ignore them. Rather, a relational focus highlights political factors and underscores them so we can address them. I can now address political factors further by turning to a discussion of social relations, and so I move on to consider social relations in terms of schooling.

Social Relations

A relational approach to knowing argues that the relationships we experience with others are both personal and social; they are what Dewey called transactional relationships. We are first of all social beings who are greatly affected by others, but we also greatly affect others right from the start. We are social beings who exist in relation to others at an intimate level as well as at a generalized level. We are selves-in-relation-with-others. There is a direct link between our individual subjectivity and our general sociality.

The implications of a transactional view of selves-in-relation-to-others are many. For one, we cannot focus just on the individual student, or even the student-teacher relationship, at a personal level alone, for we must take into consideration the larger social context in which both student and teacher are embedded. All of us are historical, locally situated beings. As soon as we widen our lens to take into consideration the larger social context placed within a historical timeframe, all sorts of exciting possibilities become available to us. With a larger social and historical context, we now have a variety of perspectives from which to choose. We now can have a greater understanding of our own situatedness, for we can compare ourselves to others. Others draw attention to themselves and us, through their differences, for while they may have much in common with us, they also are irreducibly distinct and different from us. They offer us contrasting images, they cause ruptures in our understanding, and they cause discontinuities. These contrasts others offer allow us the chance to become more conscious of who we are and more self-reflective. These contrasts also expose us to other possibilities and differences and help to stimulate our ideas of what is possible. Then we can even change something about ourselves that we do not like. We can grow and develop further; we can enlarge our thinking, as Benhabib says.[11]

Paradoxically, at the same time that a relational approach to knowing and education implies that schools need to offer students and teachers ways to develop caring relationships by lowering the student-teacher ratio and increasing the time students and teachers have with each other, it also implies that students need to be exposed to diversity. A relational approach to knowing argues that we learn more about our own situatedness by having ourselves reflected back to us by others not like us. As Cris Mayo argues in this volume, the more variety and differences in the others we are exposed to, the more perspective we will be able to gain on ourselves. Since we begin our lives as immature individuals who have not developed a sense of self yet, we are exposed to our culture before we are able to critique the culture we are exposed to. As Jim Garrison says, culture has us before we have it.[12] We become acculturated by the others who care for us. That acculturation process happens unconsciously, automatically, so that we are not even aware that it is taking place. Thus, when we begin to interact with others not like us, we begin with an assumption that others are like us, not even realizing the concept of difference. As Biesta points out in this volume, we become aware of our differences through our interactions with others, through our efforts to establish common meanings so that we can communicate and relate to each other, and all the mishaps and miscommunications we experience along the way. It is others not like us who help us become more conscious and aware of our own contextuality. They wake us up and make us notice what before we had taken for granted.[13]

Therefore, while I recommended that students need to experience small classroom sizes in the previous section, I also want to say that students need to experience diverse perspectives. What does it mean "to experience diverse perspectives"? There are many levels and degrees of diversity. Placing any two students together will create diversity, for there will be differences between the two, even if they come from the same family, as any siblings and even twins can attest to. Two students from two different families already walk into a classroom with a great deal of diversity, as well as commonality, between them. Add in differences in ages or make the classroom coeducational and we now have more differences that will be represented. If the students come from different socioeconomic backgrounds, then even more differences will be represented, and that's without even introducing differences due to religious and ethnic backgrounds. Because the United States is a very diverse country with people who have immigrated here from all over the world, it is not so difficult to find classrooms with a small number of students in them (twenty) who will still represent a lot of diversity. Even in more isolated parts of the country, or in other countries that are more homogenous, it is still the case that there will be differences represented that can teach us a lot. Yet it is possible to import still more differences into a small classroom community by assuring that diversity is represented in the curriculum. Maybe recommending small classroom sizes that are diverse is not quite so difficult after all. What it requires is the embracing of a multicultural curriculum.

What do I mean by "a multicultural curriculum"? Sonia Nieto's *Affirming Diversity* is an excellent source for considering the concept of multicultural education. Her book is used in many college classrooms across the United States that focus on helping future teachers understand what a multicultural curriculum should entail.[14] While I have disagreements with some of Nieto's theory—in particular her Marxist critical theory, which risks sliding into a God's-eye view of how the world should be transformed—I do think her definition of multicultural education represents a fine example of what a relational approach to knowing and education implies. Nieto does not recommend that students should enroll in a class on various cultures during the time they are matriculated in schools. She does not recommend we only study various cultures, for example, during Black History month, or Latino, Native American, or Women's History month. Nieto defines a multicultural curriculum as one that is basic and pervasive and for all students, in that culture becomes a significant way for framing all subject areas taught each day. Students should not just learn about other cultures in their foreign language classes, but in their English, science, history, math, and geography classes as well on a daily basis. In all subject areas culture should not be just a "tag on" that we add at the end of each chapter, as a supplemental text, but rather, culture should be used to frame the way we learn about the subject areas.

Following her advice, students will not just learn about the American Revolutionary War, but they will learn various perspectives of the Revolution: the British, the Founding Fathers, the indigenous tribes that lived in the area, the black slaves of the Founding Fathers, and the Founding Fathers' wives, as well as the non–property owners working in America at the time. The more worldviews introduced into a subject area, the more students will become conscious that there are differences in opinions and a variety of experiences. Teaching subject areas through a cultural lens allows students to gain a greater awareness of their own embeddedness, as well as greater understanding of others. Importantly, a multicultural curriculum offers students ways to learn how to critique the various viewpoints represented, including the majority view that is easily taken for granted and allowed to remain invisible as the established norm against which other worldviews are measured.

Nieto defines a multicultural education as one that teaches students to be critical thinkers able to critique the very curriculum they are taught. By teaching students subject areas through a cultural framing, they become aware of the situatedness of the various subject areas themselves. They learn not only about science, but also that science is influenced by different schools of thought and that there is more than one way to view science. They learn that scientific theories have changed and developed over time as scientists have gone through paradigm shifts, thus not only helping students critique past scientific theories but also making them aware that the current theories of science they are learning will change over time as well. Students learn not only the situatedness of the various subject areas they study, but also the limitations of their various sources of knowledge, their teachers—including their schoolteachers—and their texts. A multicultural curriculum teaches students about situated truths that are qualified by as much evidence as we can offer. A multicultural curriculum teaches students that criteria and standards for judging the evidence we offer change over time and can be corrected and improved on. A multicultural curriculum teaches students that the world in which we live is a pluralistic world supported by a variety of truths. It does not represent our struggles to gain knowledge as leading us to one final answer on which in the end we will all agree.[15]

We can therefore anticipate the kinds of worries a recommendation of teaching through a multicultural curriculum might trigger. Many concerns will center on fears of relativism. People worry that teaching students through a multicultural curriculum will lead them to become cynical and critical of all sources once they realize no source has the Truth and all the Answers. They worry that schoolteachers will loose students' respect and their authority, as teachers will be undermined if students are taught that their teachers cannot serve as a final source of knowledge. Some also worry that whole cultures will be undermined, for students will question the very culture their teachers, including their parents, are trying to teach them. Many fear that teaching a multicultural curriculum will incite the youth to civil disobedience, and it will lead to chaos and the undermining of basic social values (of which Socrates was accused by Athenians).

Awareness of diversity highlights our own fallibility. It emphasizes that none of us has a God's-eye view of the world; we are all embedded and embodied within the world. None of us are absolute authorities, including our schoolteachers. A relational (e)pistemology implies that we must change the way we view our teachers. They can no longer be viewed as the experts they have been historically portrayed as (I am pointing here to the topic of authority, which Charles Bingham addresses in his chapter in this volume). Teachers become other inquirers, along with students. Teachers become facilitators, resources, and guides, but not expert authorities. At the same time, teachers are still able to critique existing knowledge, as are students. Teachers and students become social critics, able to deconstruct and reconstruct, and offer new theories and contribute to the constructing of new knowledge with the help of others.

Others worry that in teaching students about diverse perspectives they will lack a commonality and cohesiveness that pulls them together as citizens. If we emphasize our differences and strangeness, the irreducibility of our alterity, how can we ever hope to learn how to work together with each other and establish grounds of commonality, on which communities depend? And, if we teach students diverse curriculums, how will we give them a common base of knowledge from which to be able to relate and communicate with each other? Still others worry that in teaching a multicultural curriculum, there are only going to be so many perspectives we can include, simply due to lack of time, not to mention lack of resources and knowledge. So which ones will we include and which ones will we leave out? For every worldview we include in our curriculum, there is another one we must leave out. On what grounds will we decide? For decide we must.

A relational education and (e)pistemology, with its emphasis on social relations, highlights our similarities with others as well as our differences. It highlights how each of us is uniquely affected by our cultural surroundings, while at the same time emphasizing that all of us share that commonality of cultural influences. A relational approach to knowing underscores our limitations and contextuality, while at the same time pointing out that all of us are limited, contextual beings, thus showing how much we also share in common. A relational (e)pistemology is a humbling approach to knowing that insists we must always reconsider the criteria we use to make curriculum decisions about what to include and what to leave out. We must always remind our students and ourselves that we are not able to be all-inclusive, and that there are many worldviews worthy of our consideration that are beyond our reach. At the same time, we must help our students learn how to critique various perspectives, once they have attempted to generously understand them, for some ideas are worth rejecting. Our theories of knowledge are qualified by as much evidence as we can socially muster, so that it is not the case that we must accept anything as good, and yet at the same time we cannot accept anything as certain, fixed, and final. A relational approach to knowing helps us critique cultural influences and avoid social determinism, while at the same time our transactional relationships with others remind us that we are not alone: We are social-beings-in-relation-with-others, thus avoiding solipsism as well.

Conclusion

I focused this chapter on some specific recommendations for schools that a relational approach to knowing implies in terms of personal and social relations, in order to help us begin to explore how our schools might look if we see them through a relational lens. The specific recommendations I made include:

Teachers need to establish caring relationships with their students.

All students need to be exposed to diversity through a multicultural curriculum.

I agree with psychoanalytic scholars that all of us begin our lives already in relation with our biological mothers and that this time extends into the early years of our lives with our childcare providers. Psychoanalytic scholars help us understand that we develop a "core identity," as Jane Flax calls it, a "voice," even a multivarious, or fractured one through our personal relationships with others. These others are like us and not like us in many ways. The ways in which they are the same and different from us help us develop our identities and make us more aware of our own context and differences. With that awareness come chances for us to critique and change ourselves.

In agreement with Nel Noddings, I have argued that the need for caring personal relationships with others extends into school settings with teachers and other students. Experiencing caring personal relationships in schools gives students chances to further develop their voices by enlarging their social contexts beyond the boundaries of their immediate families and childcare providers. Extending the diversity of voices students are exposed to even further through a multicultural curriculum increases the ranges of social contexts and offers students even more chances to become stable in their self-identities as well as better able to critique and change themselves. I tried to bring out tensions and concerns people have about teachers establishing caring relations with students as well as with teachers teaching a multicultural curriculum. These concerns center on fears of social determinism and relativism, for example. They point us to the powerful impact relations have on our lives and underscore their dangers. However, I did not point to these dangers so that we could draw the conclusion that relations should be ignored or diminished. Rather, I pointed to dangers in relations so these dangers could serve to help remind us and emphasize for us the importance of considering carefully the kinds of relationships our children experience in schools and the quality of the curriculum to which they are exposed.

If this discussion has helped to connect theory with practice, enhance the reader's understanding of the relational theories presented in other chapters as well as within this chapter, and demonstrate the kinds of impact a relational approach to knowing can have for our daily living, in particular our schools, then I have achieved my goals. How we teach our children has such a profound affect on how they will relate to the world as adults.

Notes

1. From introduction to Barbara Thayer-Bacon, *Relational "(e)pistemologies"* (New York and London: Peter Lang Publishers, 2003). Parts of this chapter are derived from Chapter 9 of *Relational "(e)pistemologies"* as well. "Transaction" is a term Dewey used late in his career in *Knowing and the Known*, with A. Bentley. Earlier in his career he used the term "interaction." Whereas "interaction" treated individuals as if they were autonomous, like billiard balls that bounce off of each other without changing each other as a result, "transaction" emphasizes that individuals are not autonomous, but are always in relation with others and are always already affecting each other as a result of their contact with each other. "Transaction" is a more fluid, porous description of individuals that emphasizes how leaky the boundaries are between individuals and others, as well as emphasizing that the relationship between individuals and others is one that is in motion (trans-action). John Dewey and Arthur Bentley, *Knowing and the Known* (Boston: Beacon Press, 1949, 1960).

2. The lower case 'e' in (e)pistemology is used to symbolize a nontranscendent epistemology, instead of a transcendent Epistemology, which I capitalize to distinguish.

3. Barbara Thayer-Bacon, *Transforming Critical Thinking: Thinking Constructively* (New York: Teachers College Press, 2000).

4. Thayer-Bacon, *Relational "(e)pistemologies,"* Chapters 1 and 2.

5. Martin Buber, *I and Thou*, 2nd ed., trans. Ronald G. Smith (New York: Charles Scribner's Sons, 1923, 1937, 1958); Simone Weil, *The Simone Weil Reader*, ed. George A. Panichas (New York: David McKay Co., Inc., 1977).

6. Jane Flax, *Thinking Fragments: Psychoanalysis, Feminism, and Postmodernism in Contemporary West* (Berkeley: University of California Press, 1990); Nel Noddings, *Caring: A Feminine Approach to Ethics and Moral Education* (Berkeley, CA: University of California Press, 1984); Nel Noddings, *The Challenge to Care in Schools: An Alternative Approach to Education* (New York: Teachers College Press, 1992); Sarah Ruddick, *Maternal Thinking: Toward a Politics of Peace* (Boston: Beacon Press, 1989).

7. Noddings, *Caring* and *The Challenge to Care in Schools*.

8. Barbara Thayer-Bacon, "The Power of Caring," in *Philosophical Studies in Education*, (Ohio Valley Philosophy of Education Society, 1997), 1–32.

9. I am an American Montessori Society (AMS) certified elementary Montessori teacher, and I taught in Montessori schools from 1981 to 1987. My own children all attended Montessori schools from around the age of three for as long as they were able to attend, depending on where we lived at the time (twenty five years total). Sources for information on the Montessori method of instruction include Maria Montessori, *The Discovery of the Child*, 2nd ed., trans. M. Josephy Costelloe (New York: Ballantine, 1972); Maria Montessori, *The Secret of Childhood*, 2nd ed., trans. M. Josephy Costelloe (New York, Ballantine, 1977), and your nearest Montessori teacher training program. Listings of teacher training programs can be found by contacting the American Montessori Society (AMS) and the International Association of Montessori Societies (IAMS).

10. Jane Roland Martin, *The Schoolhome: Rethinking Schools for Changing Families* (Cambridge, MA: Harvard University Press, 1992).

11. Seyla Benhabib, *Situating the Self: Gender, Community and Postmodernism* (New York: Routledge, 1992).
12. James W. Garrison, "A Deweyan Theory of Democratic Listening," *Educational Theory* 46, no. 4 (1996): 429–451.
13. See Maxine Greene's work for wonderful discussions on the idea of helping students become awake and aware, especially her *Teacher as Stranger: Educational Philosophy for the Modern Age* (Belmont, CA: Wadsworth Publishing Co., 1973) and *Releasing the Imagination: Essays on Education, the Arts, and Social Change* (San Francisco: Jossey-Bass Publishers, 1995).
14. Sonia Nieto, *Affirming Diversity: The Sociopolitical Context of Multicultural Education* (White Plains, NY: Longman, 1992).
15. What I describe here I have labeled elsewhere "qualified relativism." See Thayer-Bacon, "Pragmatism and Feminism as Qualified Relativism," *Studies in Philosophy and Education,* in press.

CONTRIBUTORS

Gert Biesta is professor of educational theory in the School of Education and Lifelong Learning of the University of Exeter, England (Heavitree Road, Exeter EX1 2LU, England, UK) and visiting professor for education and democratic citizenship at Örebro University, Sweden. *Derrida & Education*, Routledge, 2001, ed. with Denise Egéa-Kuehne; *Pragmatism and Educational Research*, Rowman & Littlefield, 2003, with Nicholas C. Burbules.

Charles Bingham is an assistant professor of curriculum theory at the Simon Fraser University, British Columbia, Burnaby, BC V5A 1S6, Canada. *Schools of Recognition: Identity Politics and Classroom Practices*, Rowman & Littlefield, 2001.

Jaylynne N. Hutchinson is an associate professor of cultural studies in education, Department of Educational Studies at Ohio University, Athens, OH, 45701. Her primary areas of scholarship are the radical democratic community and democratic education, diversity and difference, and narrative inquiry. *Students on the Margins*, SUNY Press, 1999.

Bonnie Lyon McDaniel has recently defended her doctoral dissertation in Educational Leadership and Policy Studies at the University of Washington, Seattle, WA 98195. Her primary areas of scholarship are philosophy of education, democratic theory, and gender studies.

Frank Margonis is an associate professor in the Department of Education, Culture & Society at the University of Utah, Salt Lake City, UT, 84112. He writes on the philosophy of pedagogy and educational policy.

Cris Mayo is an assistant professor in the Department of Educational Policy Studies and the Gender and Women's Studies Program at the University of Illinois at Urbana–Champaign, Champaign, IL 61820. Her research interests include gender and sexuality studies and educational philosophy.

Cherlyn M. Pijanowski works in the Seattle area with the Small Schools Coaches Collaborative, a joint project between the Small Schools Project, the Coalition of Essential Schools Northwest Center, and the University of Washington Center on the Reinvention of Public Education. Small Schools

Project/CES NW Center, 7900 East Green Lake Drive North, Suite 212, Seattle, WA 98103. Pijanowski's research interests include relational and democratic education, and psychoanalytic approaches to education.

Rosalie M. Romano is an associate professor in the Department of Educational Studies at Ohio University, Athens, OH 45701. Her primary areas of scholarship are democratic education, feminist epistemologies, moral and ethical dimensions of teaching, and cultural studies. *Forging an Educative Community*, Peter Lang, 2000, *Hungry Minds in Hard Times*, Peter Lang, 2002.

Alexander M. Sidorkin is an assistant professor in the Division of Educational Foundations and Inquiry, Bowling Green State University, Bowling Green, OH, 43403. His interest is in the theory of dialogue in education and the pedagogy of relations. *Beyond Discourse*, SUNY Press, 1999; *Learning Relations*, Peter Lang, 2002.

Barbara S. Stengel is professor of educational foundations at Millersville University, Millersville, PA 17551. Her primary areas of scholarship are teacher knowledge, teacher education, and the moral dimensions of teaching and learning. *Just Education: The Right to Education in Context and Conversation*, Loyola University Press, 1991.

Barbara J. Thayer-Bacon is a professor in the Program of Cultural Studies in Education, University of Tennessee, Knoxville, TN 37996. Her primary areas of scholarship as a philosopher of education are feminist theory and pedagogy, pragmatism, and cultural studies in education. *Philosophy Applied to Education*, Prentice Hall, 1998 (with Charles Bacon); *Transforming Critical Thinking*, Teachers College Press, 2000; *(Relational "(e)pistemologies,"* Peter Lang, 2003.

INDEX